LITERATURE ACTIVITIES FOR YOUNG CHILDREN

Art Projects - Skill Building Activities - Plot Summaries

Written by Dianna Sullivan
Illustrated by Dr. Diane S. Spears

HOLIDAY STORIES

Introduction and Special Note	2
The Biggest Pumpkin Ever By Steven Kroll (Scholastic, 1984)	3
Little Witch's Big Night By Deborah Hautzig (Random House, 1984)	11
It's Thanksgiving By Jack Prelutsky (Greenwillow Books, 1982)	17
sometimes it's Turkey-sometimes it's Feathers By Lorna Balian (Abingdon Press, 1973)	22
The Littlest Angel By Charles Tazewell (Ideals Publishing Corp., 1946)	28
'Twas The Night Before Christmas By Clement C. Moore (Ideals Publishing Corp, 1946)	34
The Valentine Bears By Eve Bunting (Clarion Books, 1983)	51
The Best Valentine In The World By Marjorie Weinman Sharmat (Holiday House, 1982)	41
The Mother's Day Mice by Eve Bunting (Clarion Books, 1986)	62
Leprechauns Never Lie By Lorna Balian (Abingdon Press, 1980)	70
Home For A Bunny By Margaret Wise Brown (Golden Press-Western Publishing Co., 1956)	78
The Country Bunny And The Little Gold Shoes By Du Bose Heyward (Houghton Mifflin, 1939)	87

The classroom teacher may reproduce copies of materials in this book for classroom use only. The reproduction of any part for an entire school system is strictly prohibited. No part of this publication may be transmitted, stored, or recorded in any form without permission from the publisher.

Teacher Created Materials, Inc.
P.O. Box 1214
Huntington Beach, CA 92647
©1990 Teacher Created Materials, Inc.
Made in U.S.A.
ISBN 1-55734-304-7

Introduction

Literature Activities for Young Children employs a multi-sensory approach to learning based on twelve popular children's books. This book incorporates a variety of activities to meet the needs and learning styles of young children. Many follow-up suggestions are listed and include the following:

(1) Extended Activities

- finger plays
- games, songs, and poems
- creative movement
- choral reading
- questioning techniques
- gross motor activities
- dramatic play
- show 'n' share ideas

(2) Art Activities

- stencils
- puzzles
- finger painting
- mosaics
- sponge/bleach/candle paintings
- paint blowing
- wax crayon rubbings
- tissue overlays

(3) Seatwork

- mazes
- counting
- matching sets to numerals
- sequencing
- categorizing
- hidden pictures
- rhyming
- dot to dot
- tracing
- upper and lower case letters

Special Note:

Because some art projects in this book may present too much coloring for young children, the following options may be helpful.

- Outline the character.
- Color only certain items, e.g. the hat and shoes; specify which colors to use.
- Duplicate pattern pieces onto colored construction paper.
- Have children work as a group to complete one project.
- Glue fabric scraps, paper, glitter, beans, etc. to decorate a project.

The Biggest Pumpkin Ever

By Steven Kroll

SUMMARY

Clayton and Desmond were two mice who fell in love with the same pumpkin. Clayton nurtured the pumpkin in the daytime and Desmond nurtured the pumpkin in the evening time. Neither mouse realized the other was nurturing the pumpkin. Clayton wanted the pumpkin to grow large enough to win the grand prize at the town's pumpkin contest. Desmond wanted the pumpkin to grow large enough to become the neighborhood's largest jack-o-lantern. Soon the pumpkin was ready to be harvested. Then the mice discovered that the pumpkin had been nurtured by both of them. They compromised on the use of the pumpkin. First, the pumpkin won the contest at the town's fair for the largest pumpkin; second, the pumpkin became the neighborhood's largest jack-o-lantern.

SUGGESTED ACTIVITIES

Pumpkin Directions: Give each child a large piece of paper and a box of crayons. Teacher dictates these directions: (1) Draw a red pumpkin in the top right corner of your paper. (2) Draw a blue pumpkin in the top left corner of your paper. (3) Draw a green pumpkin in the bottom center of your paper. (4) Draw 5 orange pumpkins in the center of your paper.

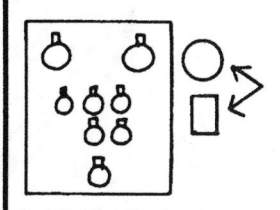

Pumpkin Patch Alphabet: Color and cut out the pumpkins on page 10. Children match the upper case pumpkins to the lower case pumpkins.

Felt Pumpkins: Cut large, medium and small pumpkin shapes from a variety of felt colors. Have children sequence the pumpkins from large to small and vice versa.

Candy Pumpkins, Corn, Jellybeans: Children match (1-1 correspondence) candy pumpkin, to a candy corn, to a jellybean.

Soap Painted Pumpkins: Put some detergent flakes, orange tempera and a little liquid starch into a container and mix. Paint pumpkin pictures. This will produce rough and bumpy pumpkins.

Name _____

The Biggest Pumpkin Ever

The Biggest Pumpkin Ever

1. Color and cut out pumpkins on pages 4-7.
2. Sequence the pumpkins from smallest to largest.
3. Staple book on left hand side of pumpkins.

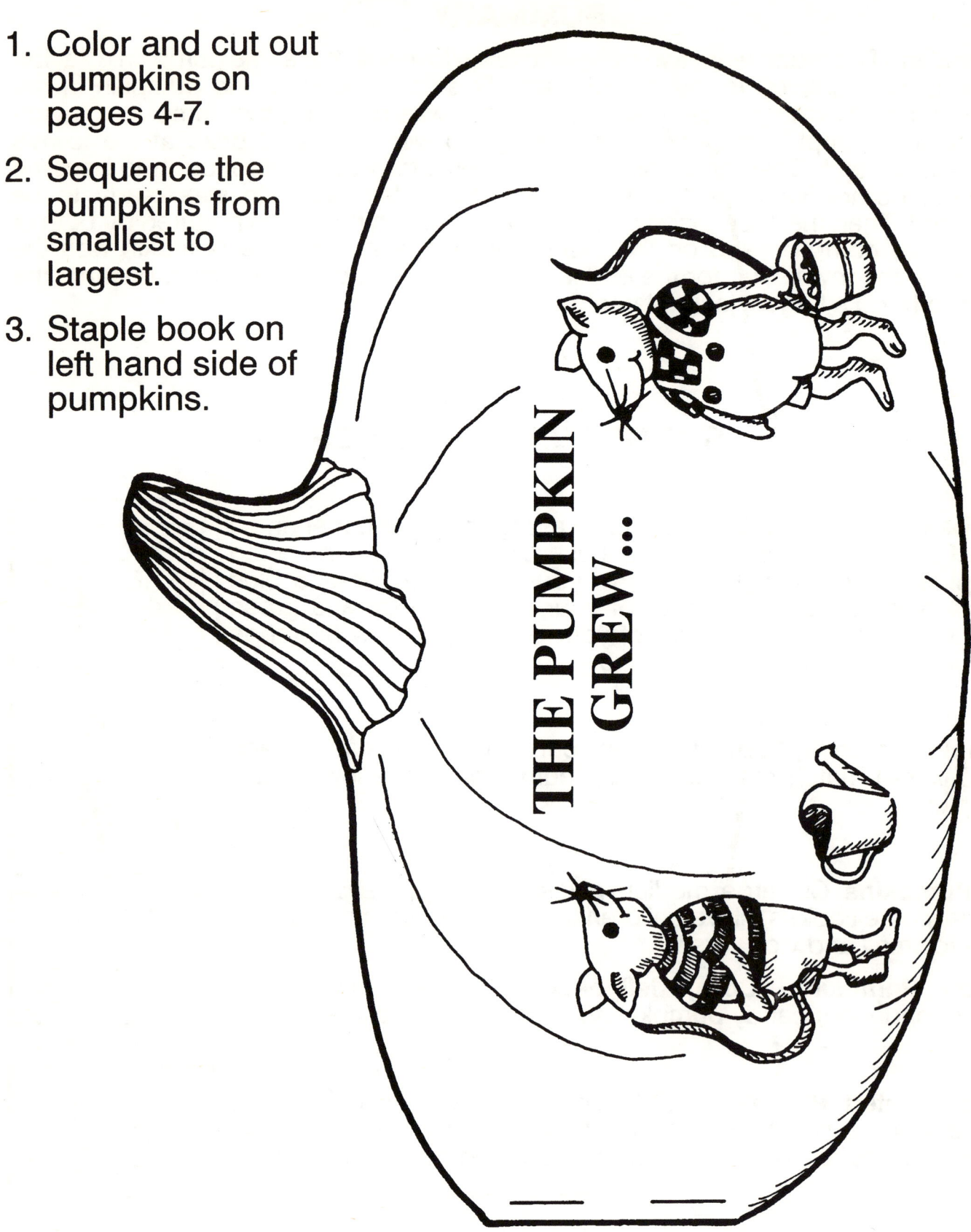

THE PUMPKIN GREW...

Name _____

The Biggest Pumpkin Ever *(cont.)*

The Biggest Pumpkin Ever

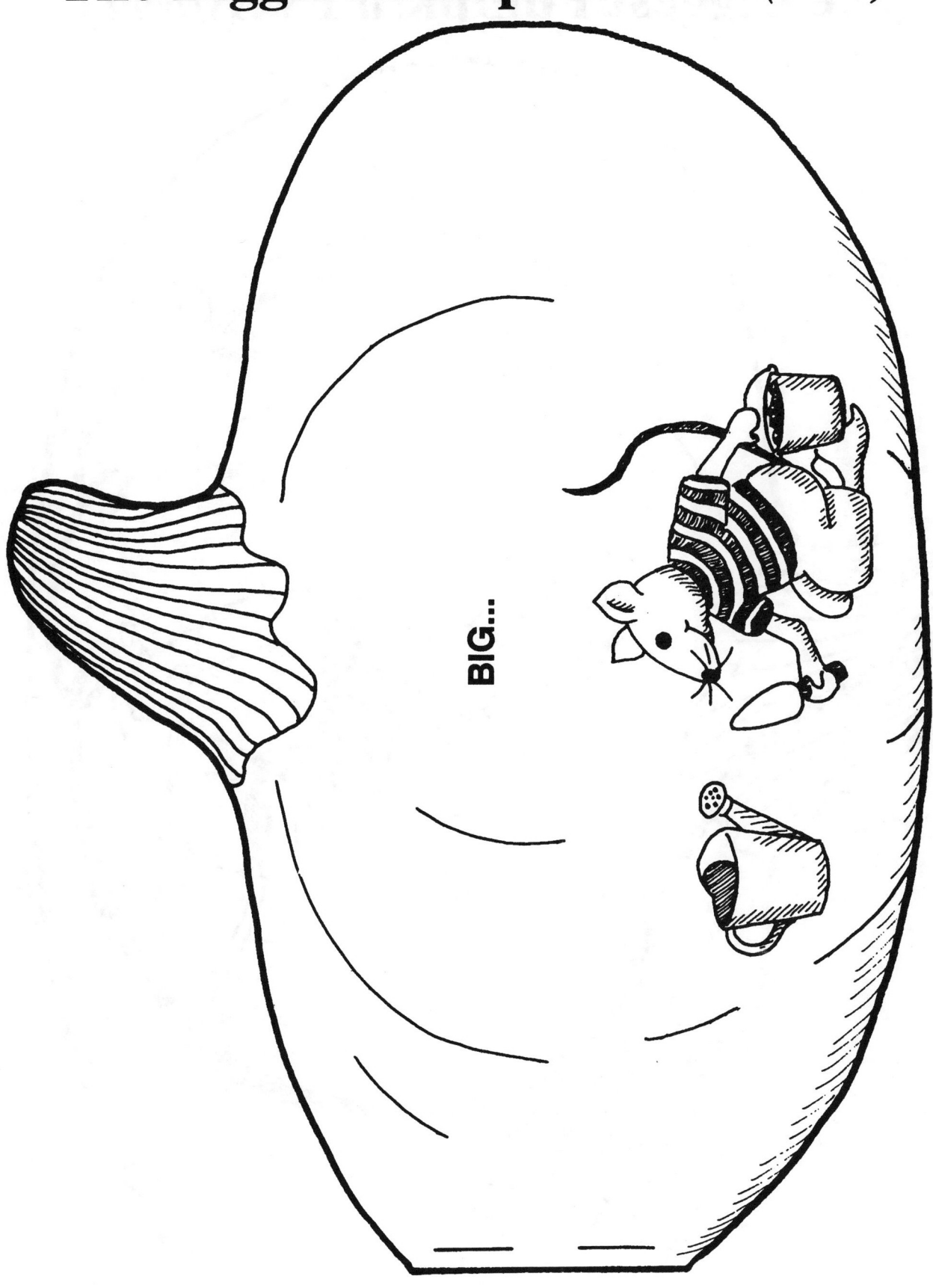

BIG...

© 1990 Teacher Created Materials, Inc. #304 Literature Activities For Young Children, Book 5

Name _____   *The Biggest Pumpkin Ever*

The Biggest Pumpkin Ever *(cont.)*

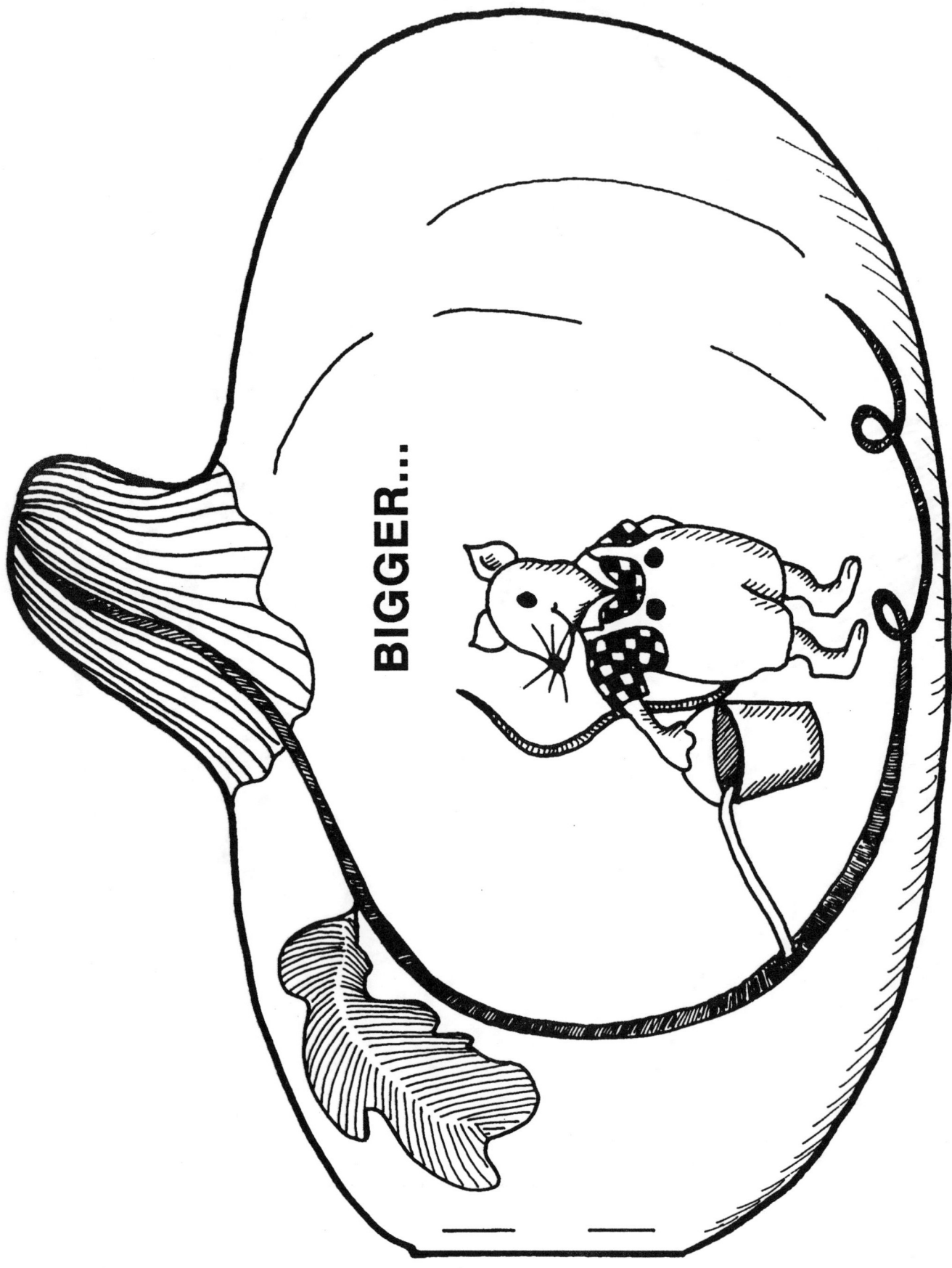

BIGGER...

Name _____

The Biggest Pumpkin Ever *(cont.)*

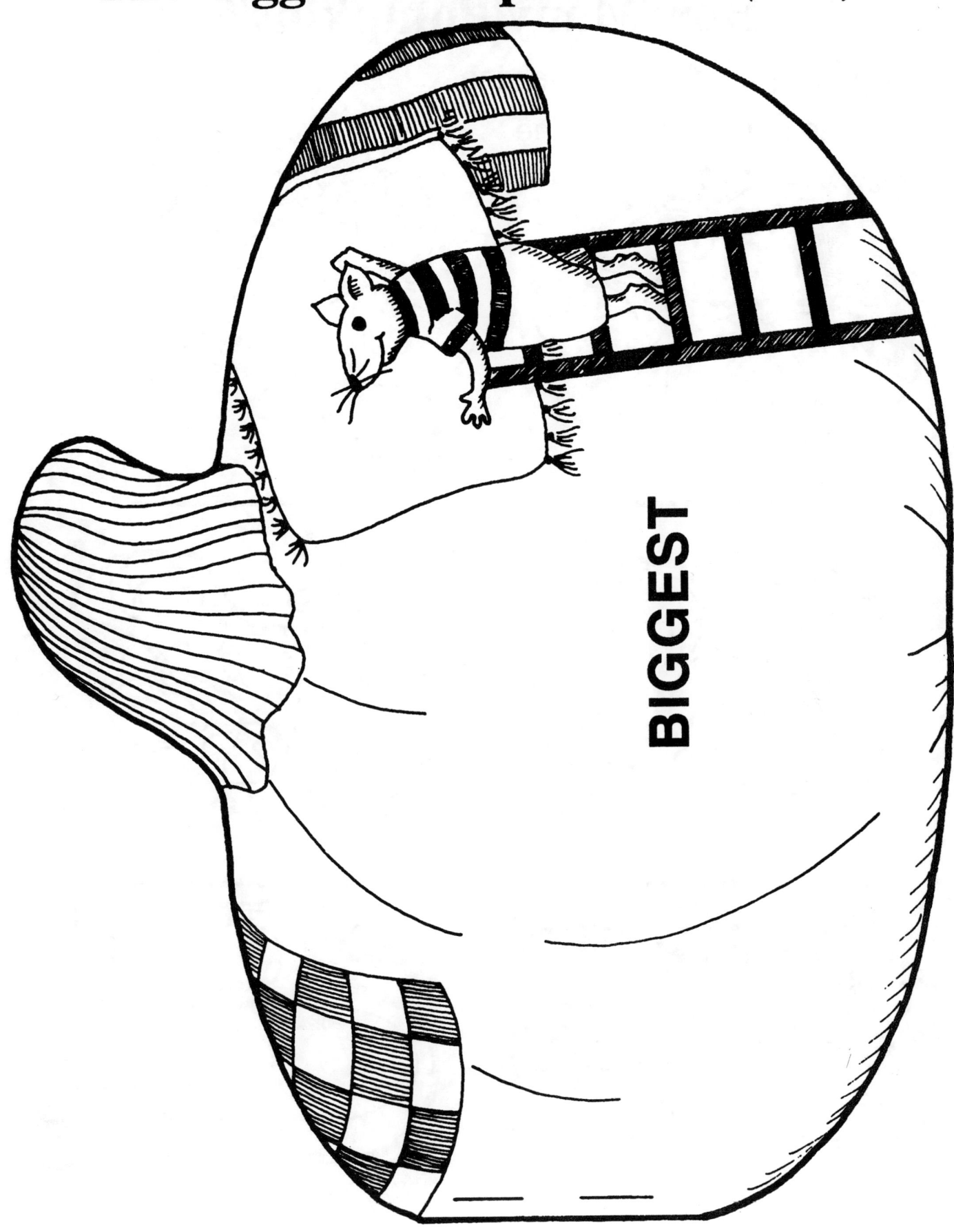

Name _____

The Biggest Pumpkin Ever

How Many Pumpkins?

1. Count the pumpkins on the vine.
2. Write the number on the line.
3. Color.

Name _____   *The Biggest Pumpkin Ever*

A Pumpkin Grows

1. Cut out the pictures and glue in order.
2. Color.

1
2
3
4

Name _____

The Biggest Pumpkin Ever

Pumpkin Matching

1. Reproduce this page two or three times.
2. Write upper case letters on some and corresponding lower case on others.
3. Color, cut out and match.

*See suggested activity page 3.

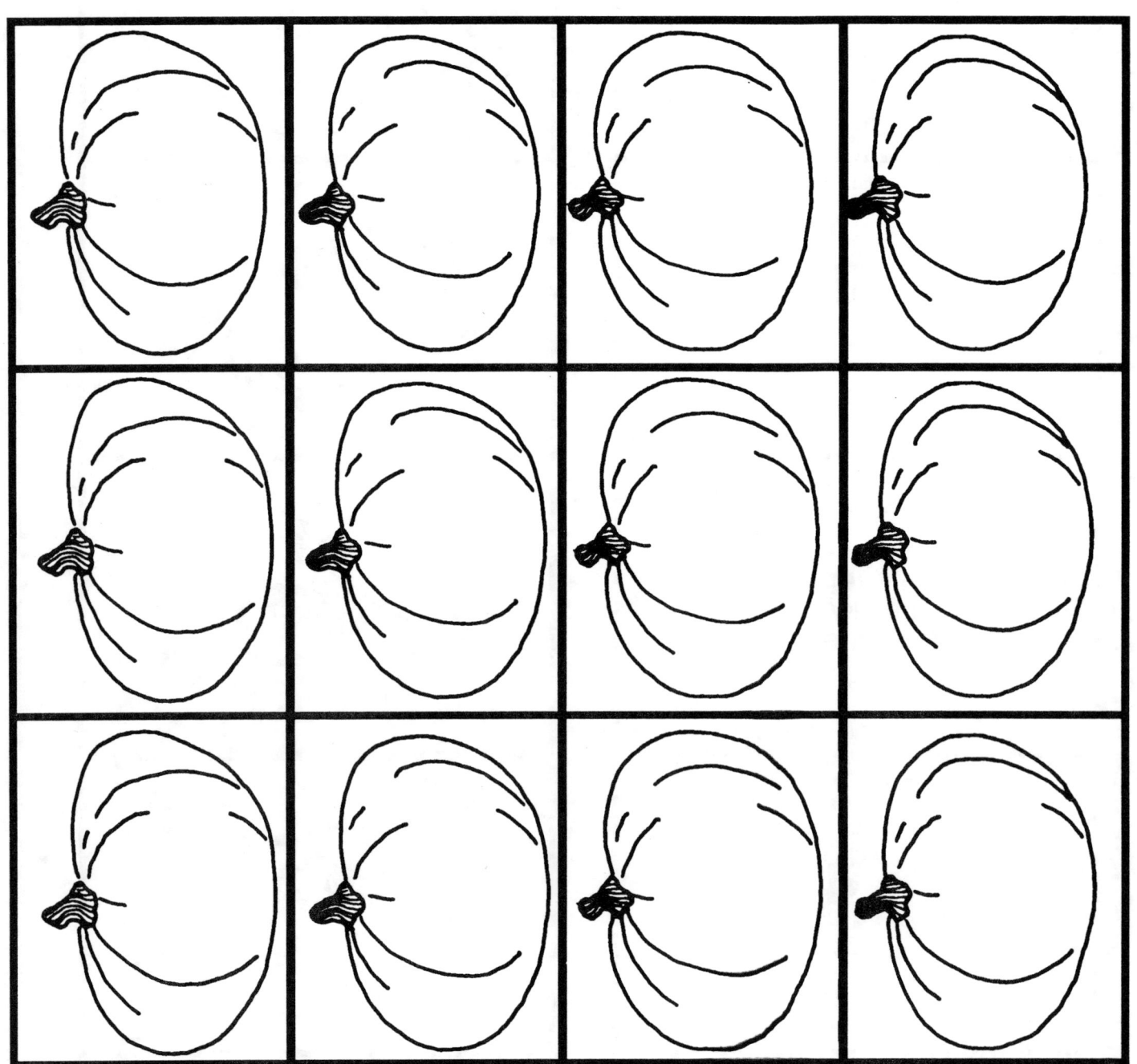

Little Witch's Big Night

SUMMARY

Little Witch cleans her room tidy and neat. Mother witch punishes her by not allowing her to go out on the Halloween ride. She is sad for awhile, but then some children who are trick-or-treating knock at her door. Since she has no candy treats, she decides to treat them each to a ride on her broom. The children have a wonderful broom ride and see many things from the sky trip. The Little Witch and the children have the best Halloween ever!

SUGGESTED ACTIVITIES

Witch's Hat And Brooms Night: Draw some black witch hats (triangle and line hat) and some yellow witch's brooms (line and funnel broom) on white construction paper. Press down hard on crayons creating heavy wax coated hats and brooms. With watered-down blue tempera paint, cover the whole paper. The hats and brooms will resist the paint and appear to be floating in the night!

Flying Witch: Blow up an orange balloon. With a black permanent marker, draw on eyes, long nose complete with wart, mouth with some blacked-out teeth and a witch's hat. Children keep balloon in the air by continually hitting it upwards.

Witch Creative Movements: Children pretend they are witches. (1) Fly through the sky on their brooms, (2) Cook a bubbly pot of toads, rats, tadpoles, etc.

Witch's Buttons: Cut out ten tagboard rectangles. Reproduce witch and her hat (page 16) ten times. Glue a witch onto each of the tagboard pieces. Cut out ten witches' hats. Write the numbers 1-10 on each of the hats. Glue the hats onto witches' heads. Laminate the boards. Provide a container of small buttons. Children place the correct number of buttons on the dress to represent the printed numeral on the hat.

Name _____

Little Witch's Big Night

Little Witch's Big Night

1. Color and cut out the witch on pages 12-14.

2. Glue the bottom half of the witch (page 13) to Tab A on the top half of the witch.

Tab A

Name _____

Little Witch's Big Night

Little Witch's Big Night
(cont.)

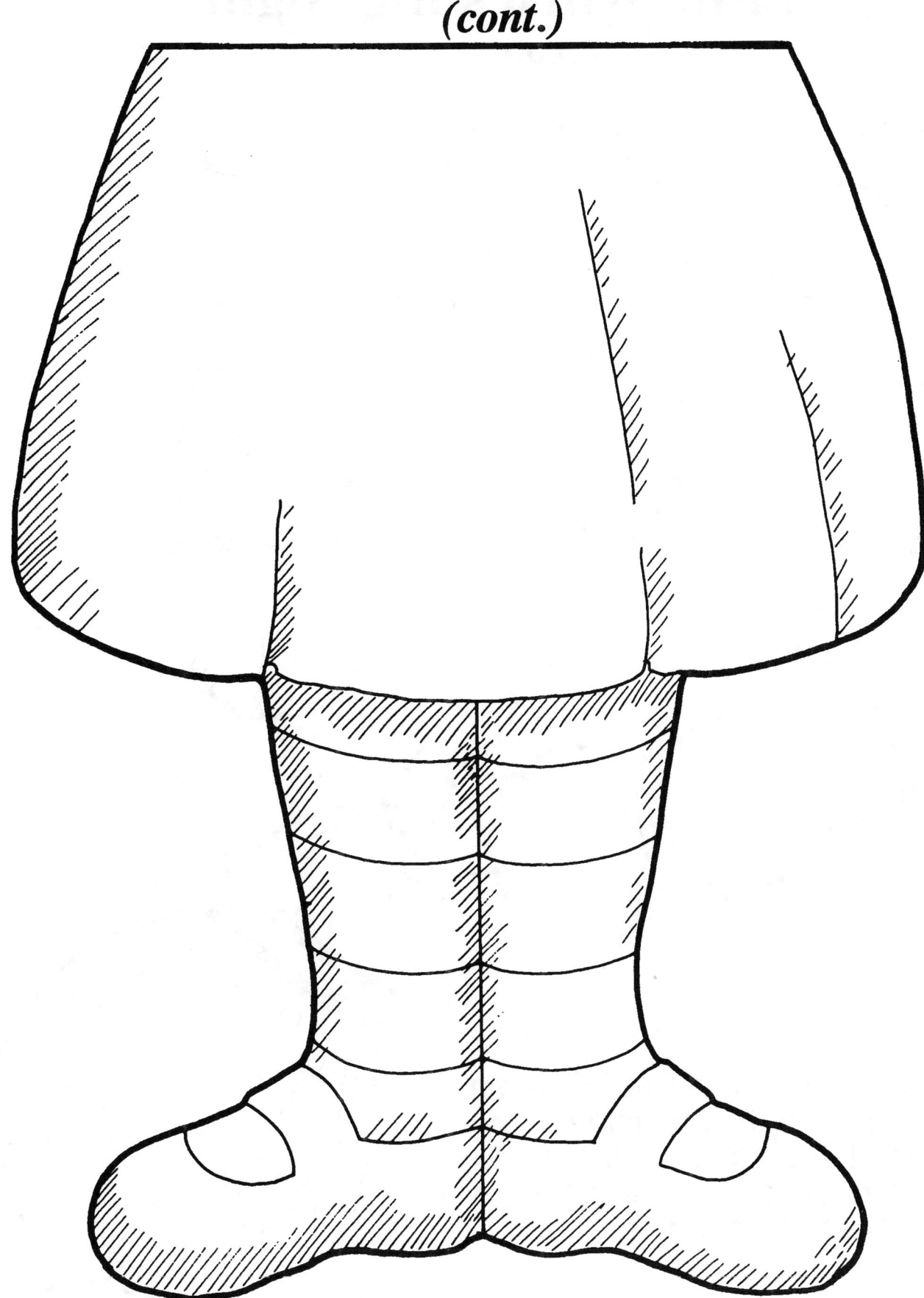

Name _____

Little Witch's Big Night
(cont.)

Tab C

Tab B

3. **Arms:** Fold Tabs B and C under. Glue tabs to the backside of the witch at shoulders. Bring arms forward. Glue hands together, with broom sandwiched between.

Name _____   Little Witch's Big Night

Things That Belong Together

1. Draw a line from the part to the whole.
2. Color.

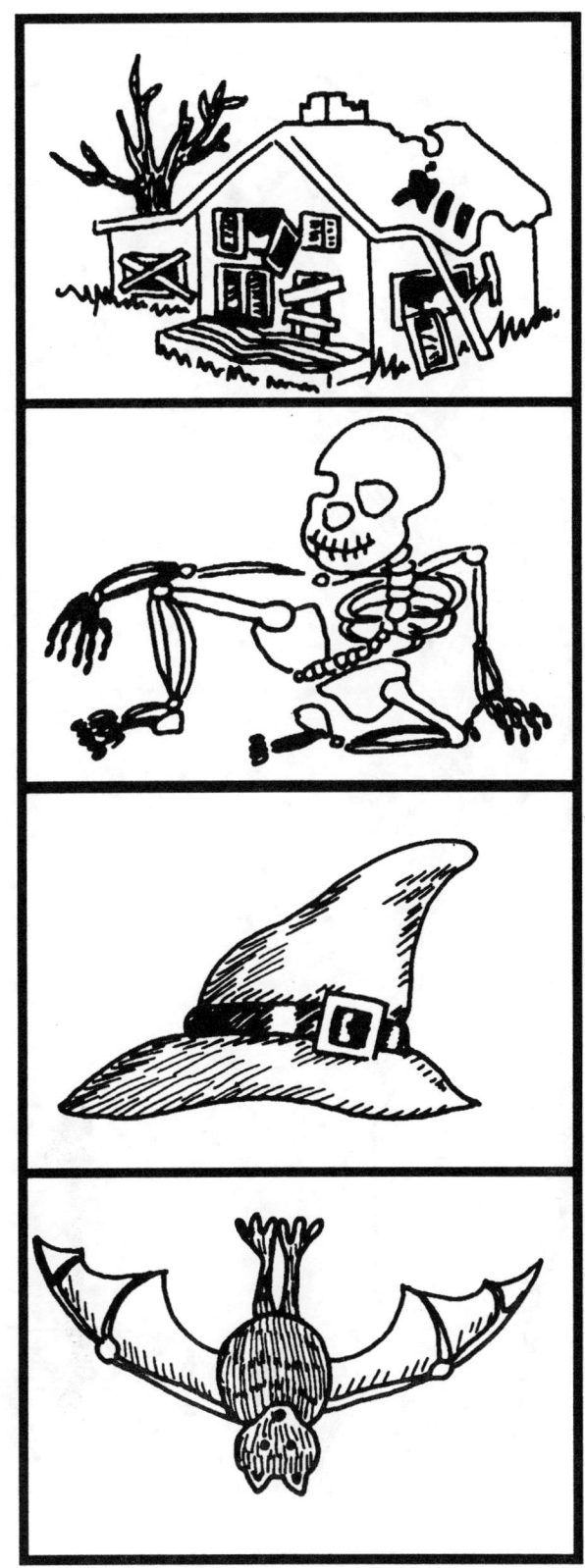

© 1990 Teacher Created Materials, Inc.   15   #304 Literature Activities For Young Children, Book 5

Name _____

Little Witch's Big Night

*See suggested activity page 11.

It's Thanksgiving

By Jack Prelutsky

SUMMARY

This book contains a collection of Thanksgiving stories told in verse. Included are stories about dinner at grandmother's house, the first Thanksgiving with the Pilgrims and Indians, what turkeys may be thinking at Thanksgiving, and a Thanksgiving Day Parade. Also described are Thanksgiving football games, the wishbone, and turkey leftovers. The stories are witty, fast moving, and very appealing to children.

SUGGESTED ACTIVITIES

Indian Corn: Pop popcorn and separate into four bags. Pour a different color powdered tempera paint into each bag and shake. Reproduce the corn pattern (page 21) onto white construction paper. Apply a thick coat of white glue inside the corn outline. Press different colors of popcorn pieces onto the outline.

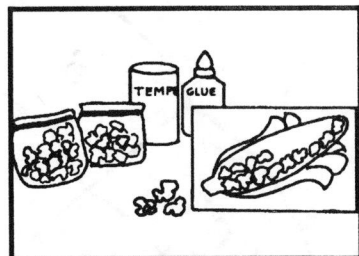

Build Log Cabins: Build some log cabins for the Pilgrim family out of wooden building logs. Make a Pilgrim family. Stand up the characters to complete the scene!

Foam Ball and Pipe Cleaner Turkey: Spray paint a foam ball brown. Let dry. Push in colored pipe cleaners for turkey feathers and feet. (Remember to spray paint outside or in a well-ventilated area.)

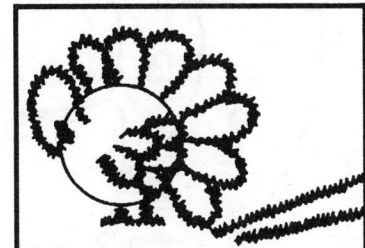

Gross Motor Movements To Thanksgiving Songs: Try doing the following movements to Thanksgiving songs: climbing, jumping, running in place or in circles, throwing, catching, skipping, dancing, calisthenics, walking in place or walking steps, using muscular strength, kicking.

Name _____   It's Thanksgiving

Colorful Turkey

Color by numbers.

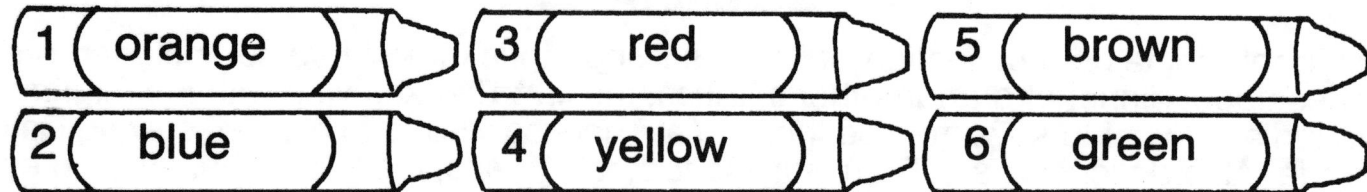

1 orange   3 red   5 brown
2 blue   4 yellow 6 green

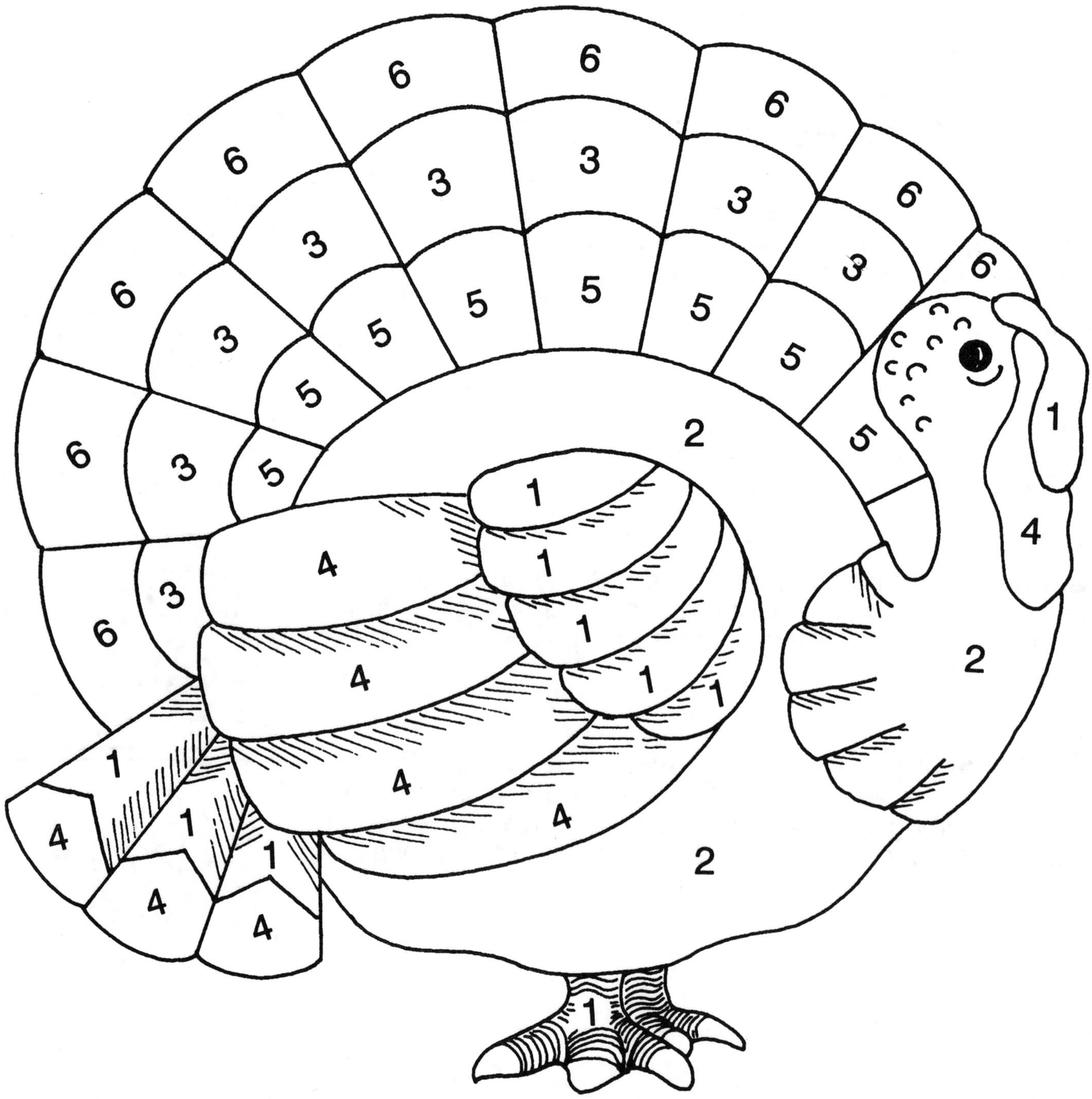

#304 Literature Activities For Young Children, Book 5   18   © 1990 Teacher Created Materials, Inc.

Name _____   It's Thanksgiving

Turkey Message

1. Find the hidden message.
2. Match the letter corn to the number blanks below.

__ __ __ __ __
3 1 7 7 11

__ __ __ __ __ __ __ __ __ __ __ __
9 3 1 6 5 8 2 4 10 4 6 2

© 1990 Teacher Created Materials, Inc.

Name _____ *It's Thanksgiving*

Hidden Turkeys

1. Find and count the turkeys.   2. Color.

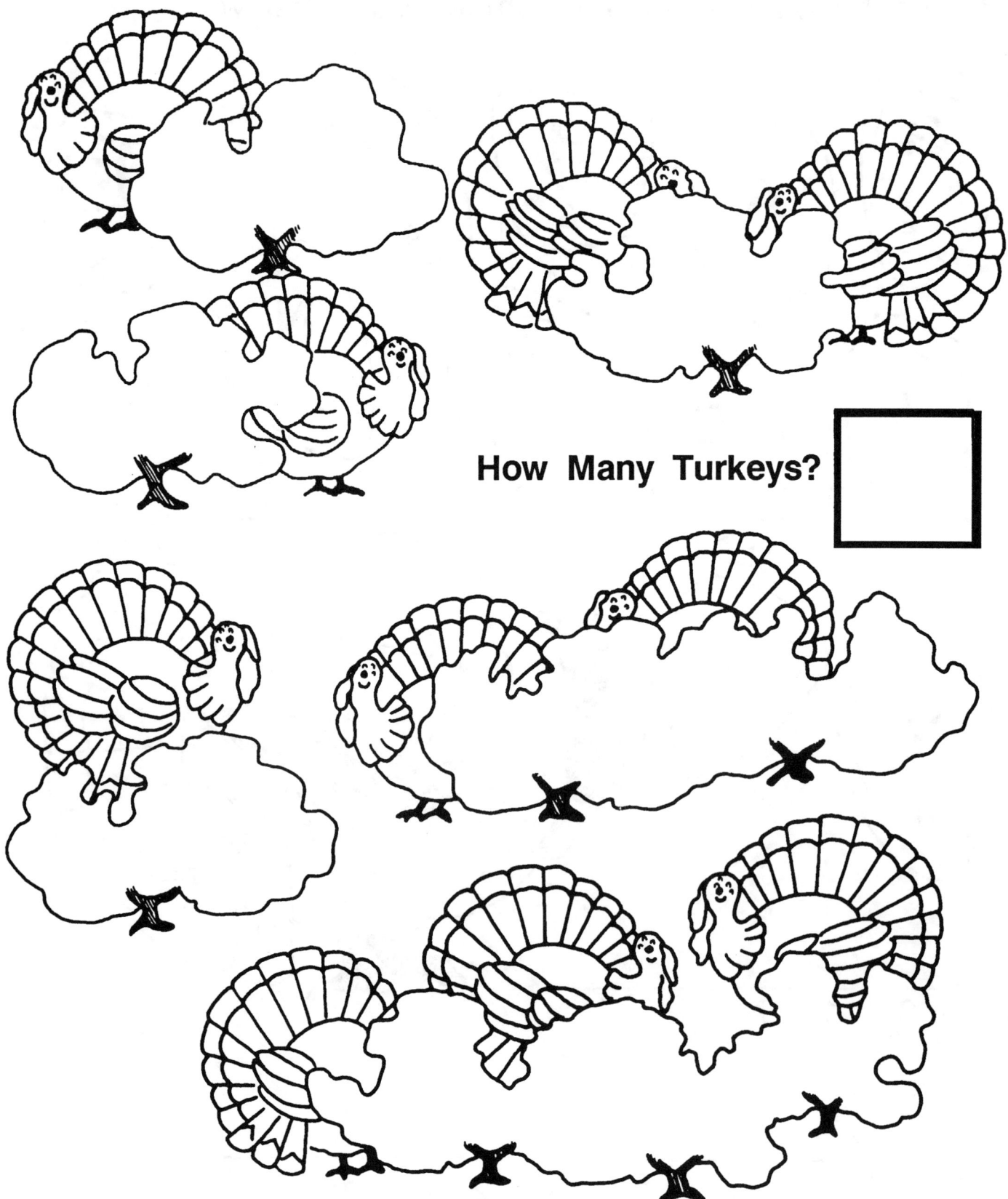

How Many Turkeys? ☐

Name _____   *It's Thanksgiving*

It's Thanksgiving

*See suggested activity page 17.

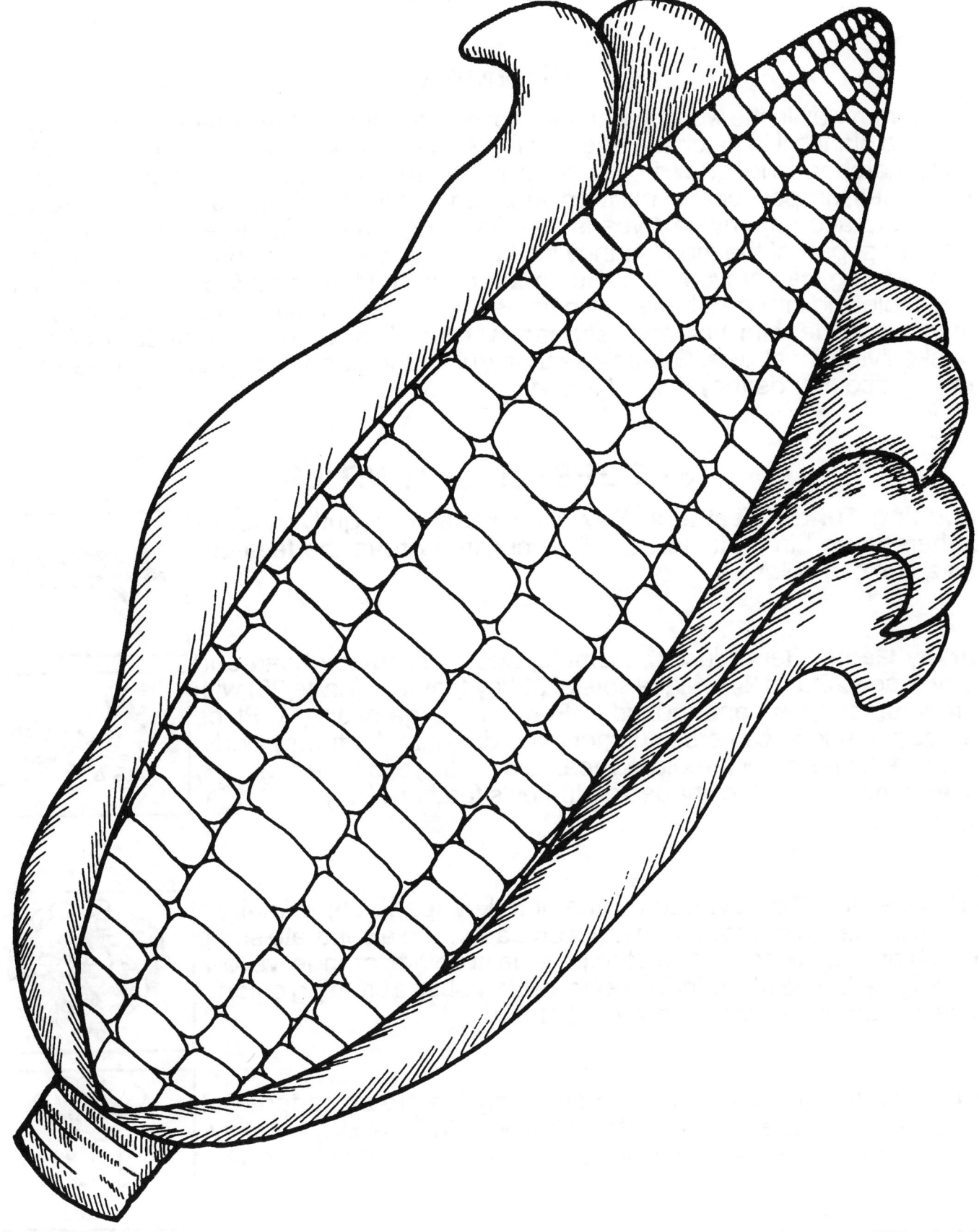

sometimes it's Turkey-sometimes it's Feathers

By Lorna Balian

SUMMARY

Mrs. Gumm was in the woods searching for mushrooms and she came across a turkey egg. She planned to hatch the egg and grow a fat turkey for her and her cat. The baby turkey hatched and grew into a fat adult turkey. As the turkey grew he ate the raspberries, grapes, beans, cat food, etc.—a lot of the foods the lady and the cat were growing to accompany next year's Thanksgiving dinner. They felt the turkey would be the best part of the meal so they let it continue eating throughout the year. At last Thanksgiving Day arrived. Mrs. Gumm prepared lots of good food. She set the cat at the table and informed him she would be back with the turkey. She took a sharpened hatchet outside with her and returned with the live turkey and all sat down to a Thanksgiving meal. Mrs. Gumm was thankful for the good food they did have and for the two nice friends they shared it with.

SUGGESTED ACTIVITIES

Grouping Turkey Feathers: Buy a package of brightly colored feathers (found in craft stores). Have children group the feathers that are like in color.

Turkey Game: Reproduce, assemble, and color turkey head and body (page 23 and 24). Make sets of turkey feathers (page 25) with numbers, shapes, and colors. Play these games: (1) Place numbered turkey feathers in numerical order onto the turkey body. (2) Make patterns with colored feathers (red, yellow, red...). (3) Make patterns with the shapes on turkey's feathers ($\bigcirc$, $\triangle$, $\bigcirc$, , $\triangle$).

String Painted Turkey: Use outline of turkey (page 26) to make a turkey shape out of brown construction paper. Dip a separate string in each of these watered down tempera paint colors: orange, yellow, red. Wiggle the painted string over the turkey shape creating colorful streaks, squiggles, lines, zig-zags. Let dry.

Turkey Golf: Paint the outside of an empty ice cream carton. Cut out a tunnel shape. Decorate the container to look like a turkey. Have children use a yardstick to hit a ball into the turkey's mouth.

Name _____

sometimes it's Turkey-sometimes it's Feathers

sometimes it's Turkey-sometimes it's Feathers

1. Color and cut out the turkey on pages 23-25.
2. Cut slits on turkey's body.
3. **Head** and **Feathers:** Fold Tabs A-L under. Push the head and feather pieces into the slits on the turkey's body. Flatten Tabs A-L.

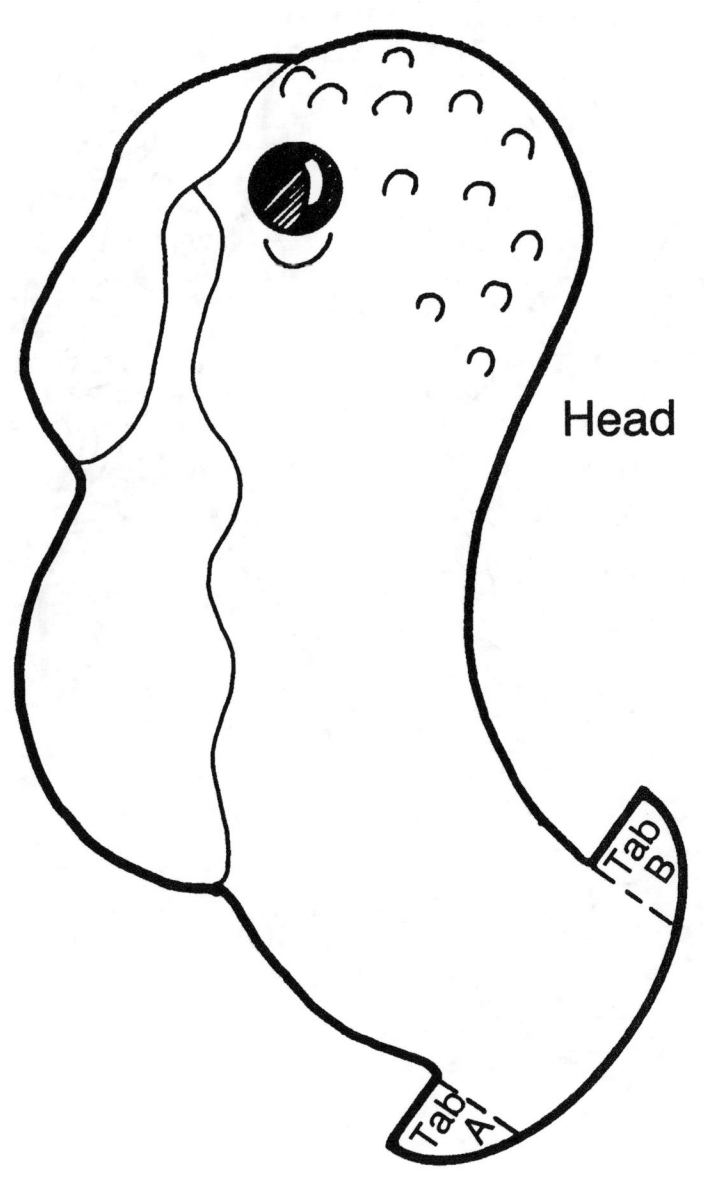

Head

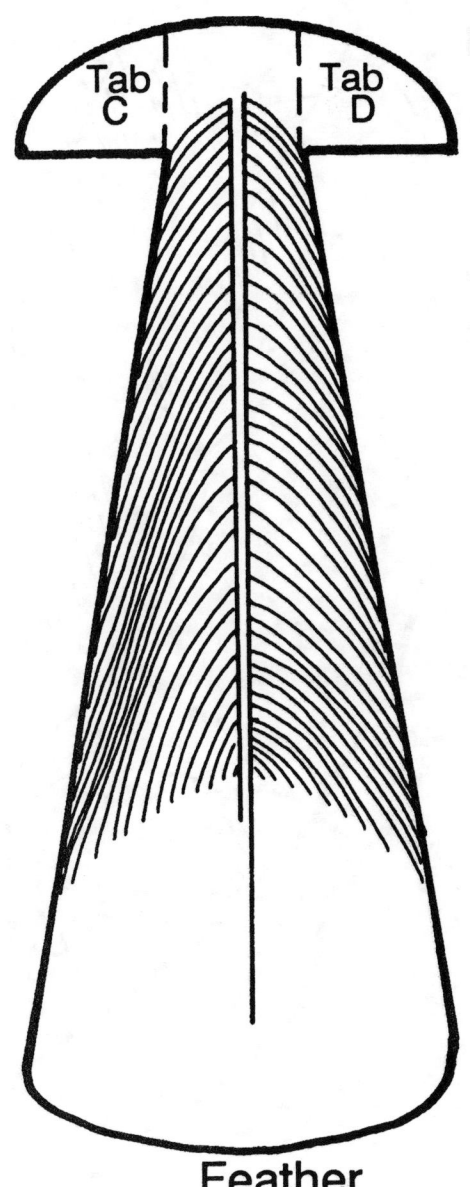

Feather

© 1990 Teacher Created Materials, Inc. #304 Literature Activities For Young Children, Book 5

Name_____   *sometimes it's Turkey-sometimes it's Feathers*

sometimes it's Turkey-sometimes it's Feathers *(cont.)*

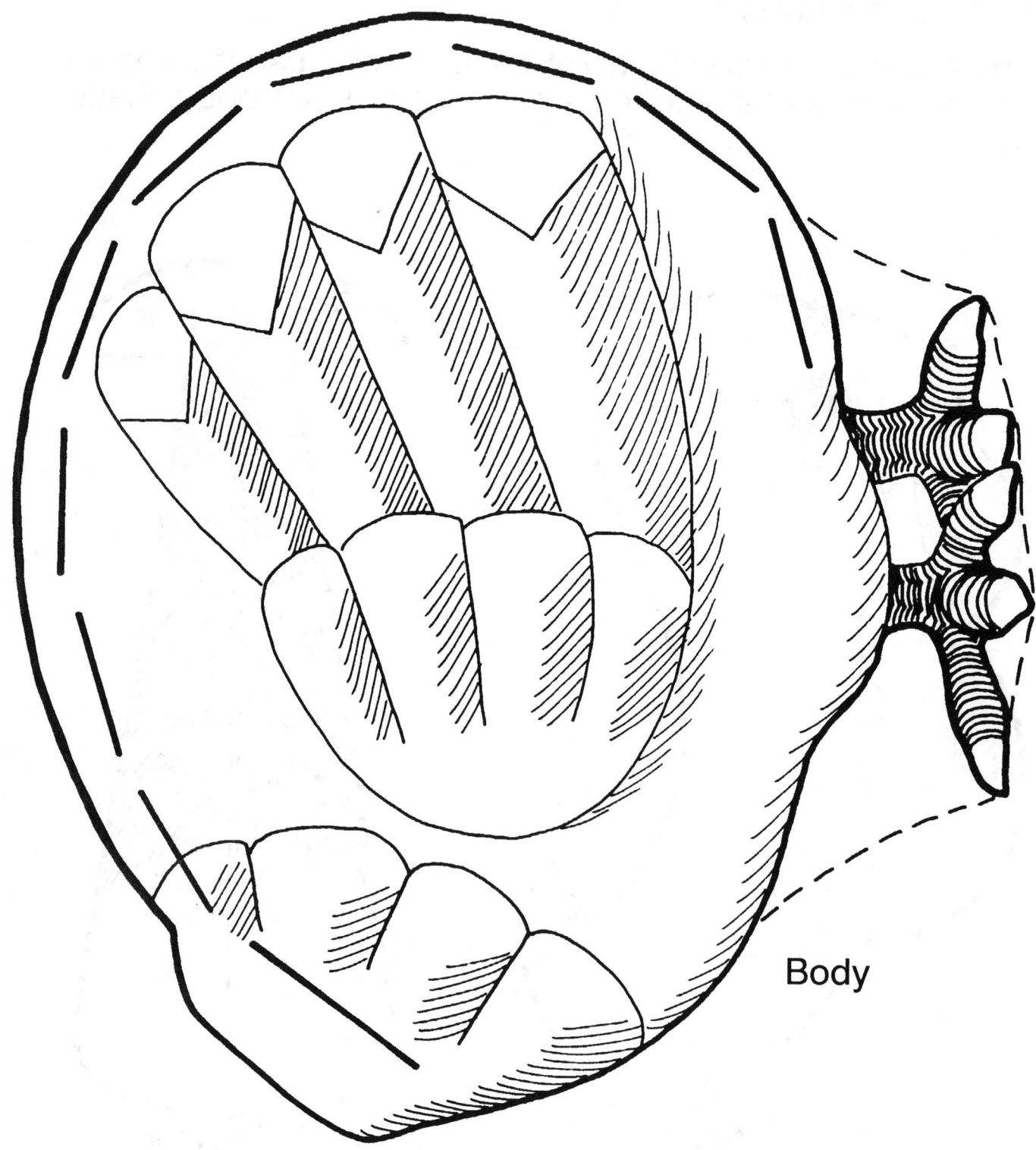

Body

Name _____

sometimes it's Turkey-sometimes it's Feathers (cont.)

Reproduce this page two times.

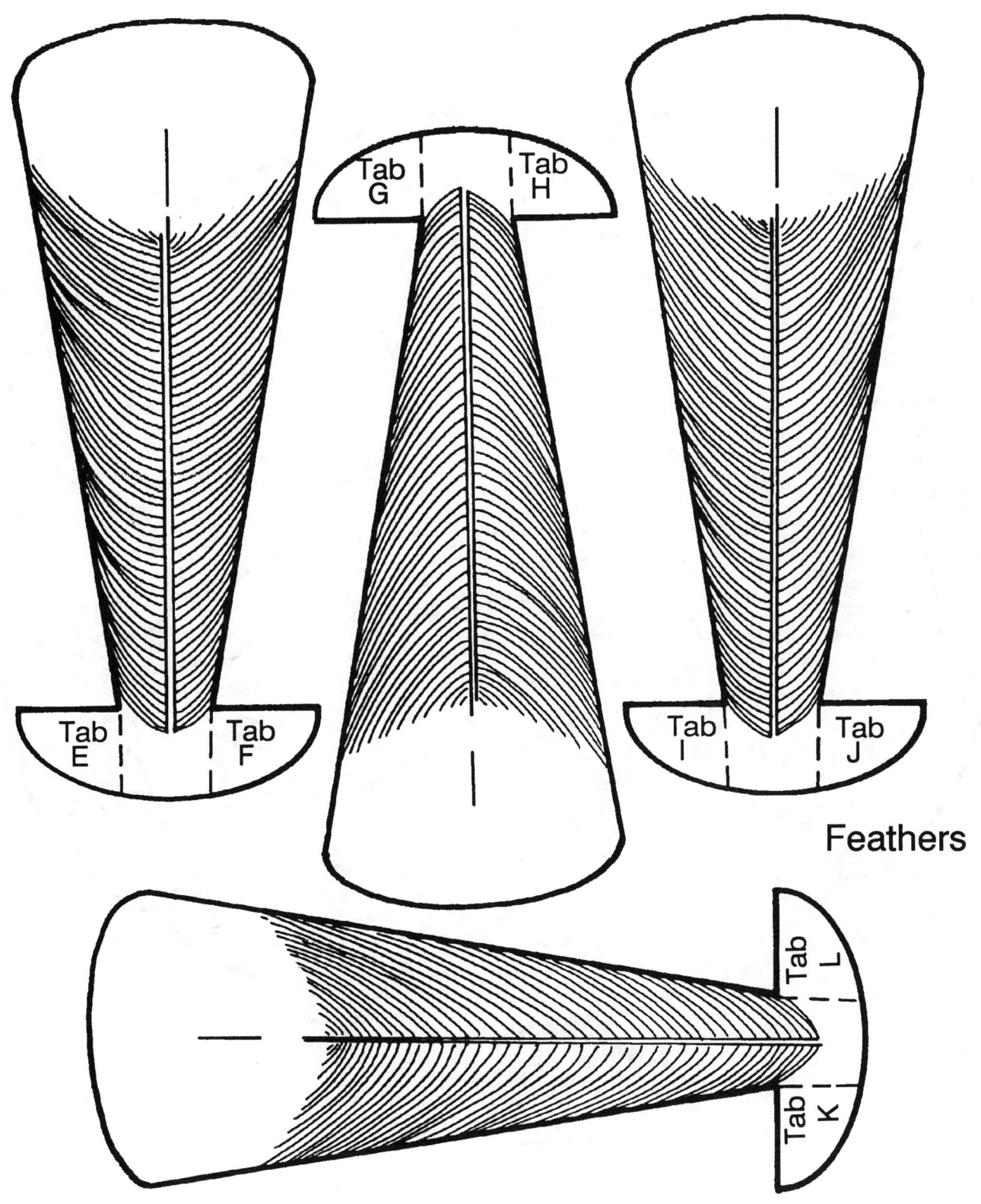

Feathers

Name_____   *sometimes it's Turkey-sometimes it's Feathers*

Matching Feathers

1. Cut and paste the dotted feathers (page 27) to the matching numbers on the turkey.
2. Color the turkey.

Name _____   *sometimes it's Turkey-sometimes it's Feathers*

Matching Feathers
(cont.)

© 1990 Teacher Created Materials, Inc.   27   #304 Literature Activities For Young Children, Book 5

The Littlest Angel
By Charles Tazewell

SUMMARY

A little four year old boy angel is very unhappy in heaven. Because of his continual naughty behavior, the little angel is sent to the Understanding Angel. The little angel promises good behavior if he can have the special wooden box from under his bed back home. The Understanding Angel grants the little angel's request.

Soon Jesus is to be born. All the angels in heaven give God a gift in honor of the birth of his Son. The little angel gives God his wooden box for baby Jesus. The box becomes the great light that overshadows the stable where Jesus is born.

SUGGESTED ACTIVITIES

Angel Sponge Printed Shapes: Cut an angel shape (use outline of angels page 32) out of several small sponges. Pour some watered-down tempera paint into flat dishes. Children dip their angel sponges into the paint and print the angel shape onto white or yellow construction paper.

Angels Painting: Glue blue tissue paper on top of white construction paper. Pour some liquid bleach into a small container. Dip a cotton swab into the bleach and then with the swab, draw angels. Make triangle bodies, circle heads, half-circle wings.

Angels Special Box: Put some objects into a big box with a lid. Cut a square out of the center of the lid. Child puts hand into the box, feels the object, describes the object to classmates, guesses what the object might be, and then looks at the object to see if he/she is correct.

Dropper Painted Angels: Fill little jars with water. Add food coloring to the jars. Draw an angel outline onto white construction paper. Children use eyedroppers to suck up the colored water and then squeeze drops of color onto the angels.

Watercolor Angels: Paint an angel picture with watercolor paints on white construction paper. Add cottonball clouds at the bottom.

Name _____

The Littlest Angel

The Littlest Angel

1. Color and cut out angel on pages 29-31.
2. Glue head Tab A, behind body page 30.
3. Glue arms onto body at dashed lines.

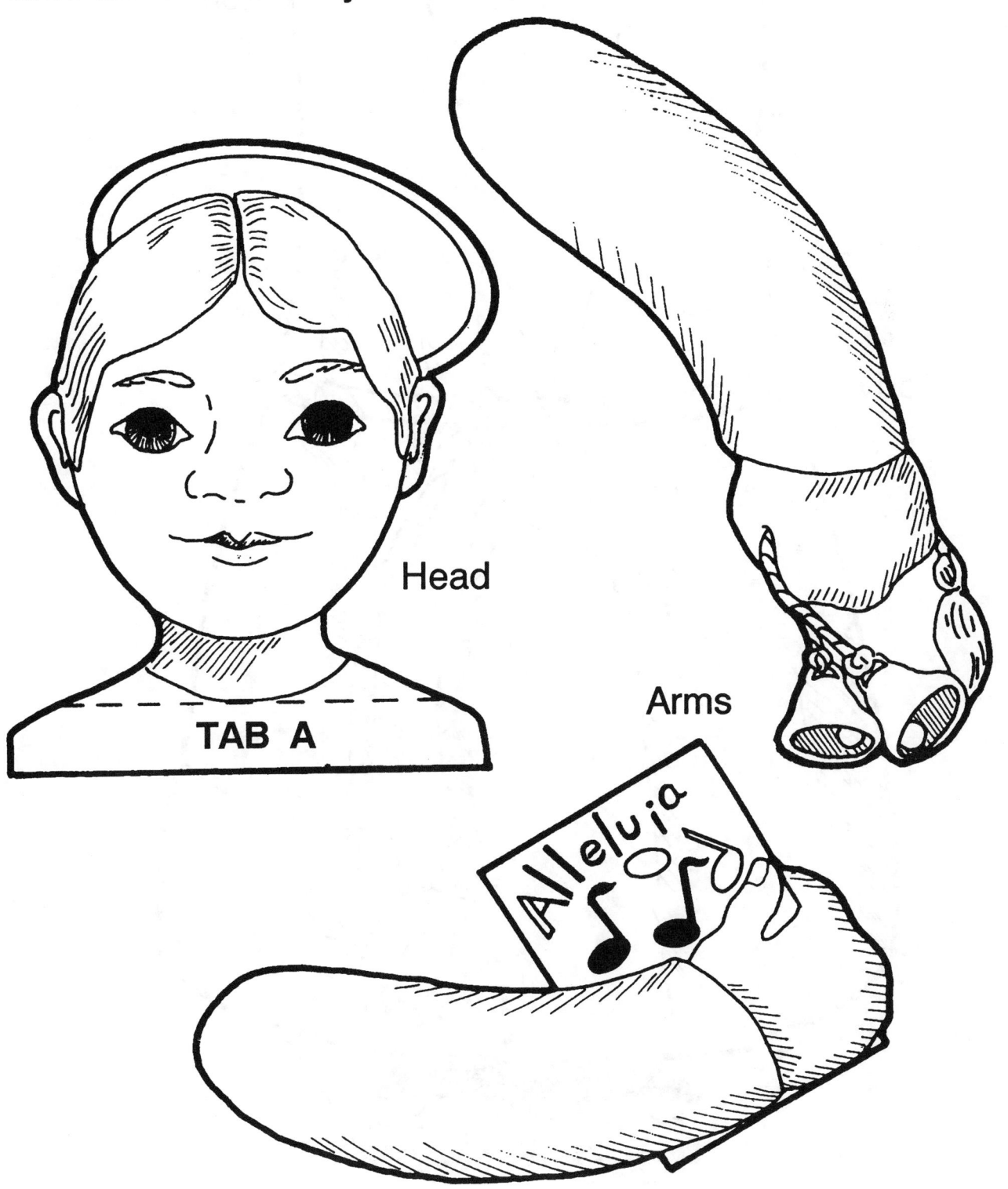

Name _____

The Littlest Angel

The Littlest Angel *(cont.)*

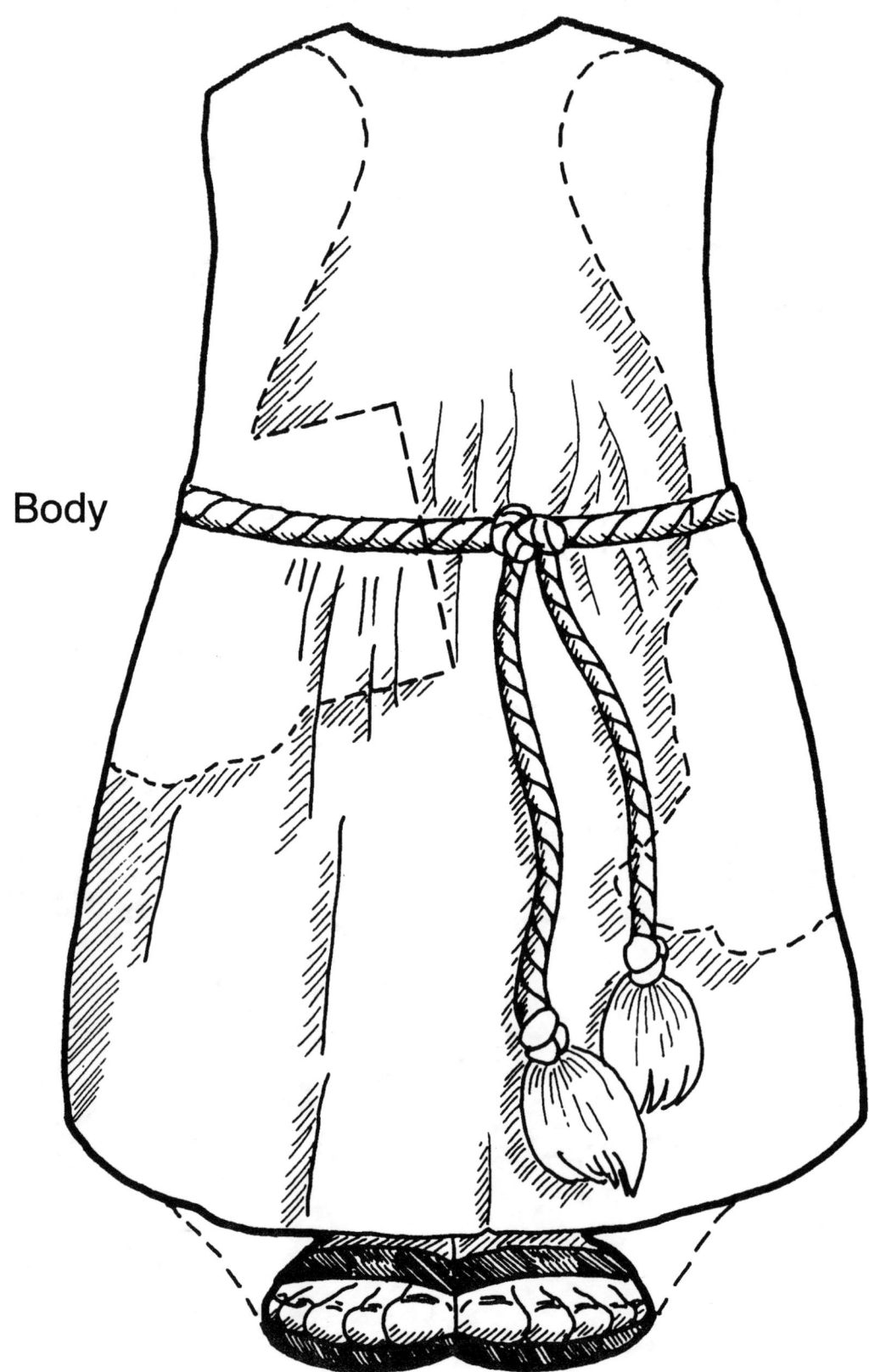

Body

#304 Literature Activities For Young Children, Book 5

Name _____

The Littlest Angel

The Littlest Angel *(cont.)*

4. Glue the angel onto the wings.

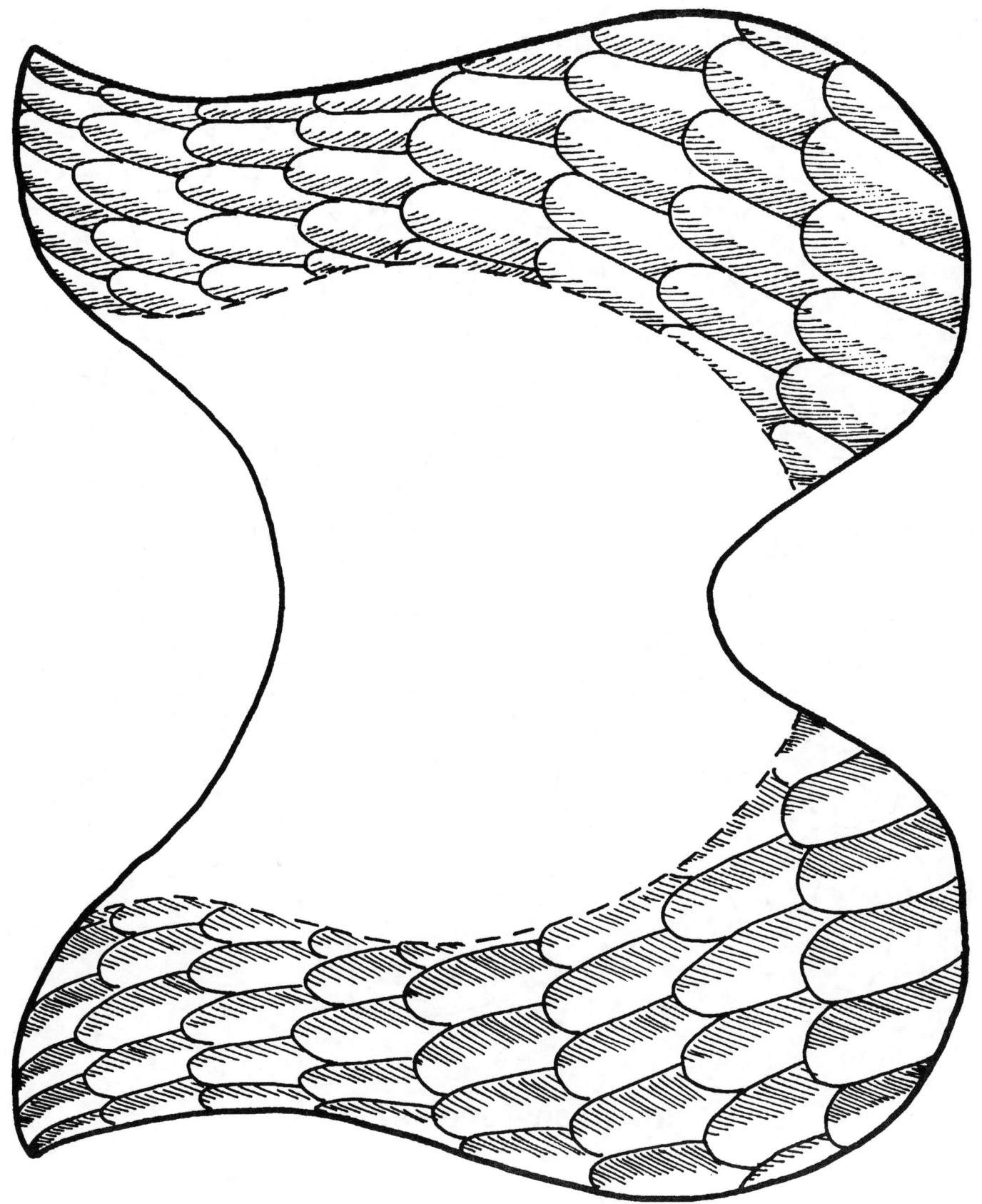

© 1990 Teacher Created Materials, Inc.   #304 *Literature Activities For Young Children, Book 5*

Name _____ The Littlest Angel

How Many Angels?

1. Trace the numbers.
2. Write a number in each angel 3-10.

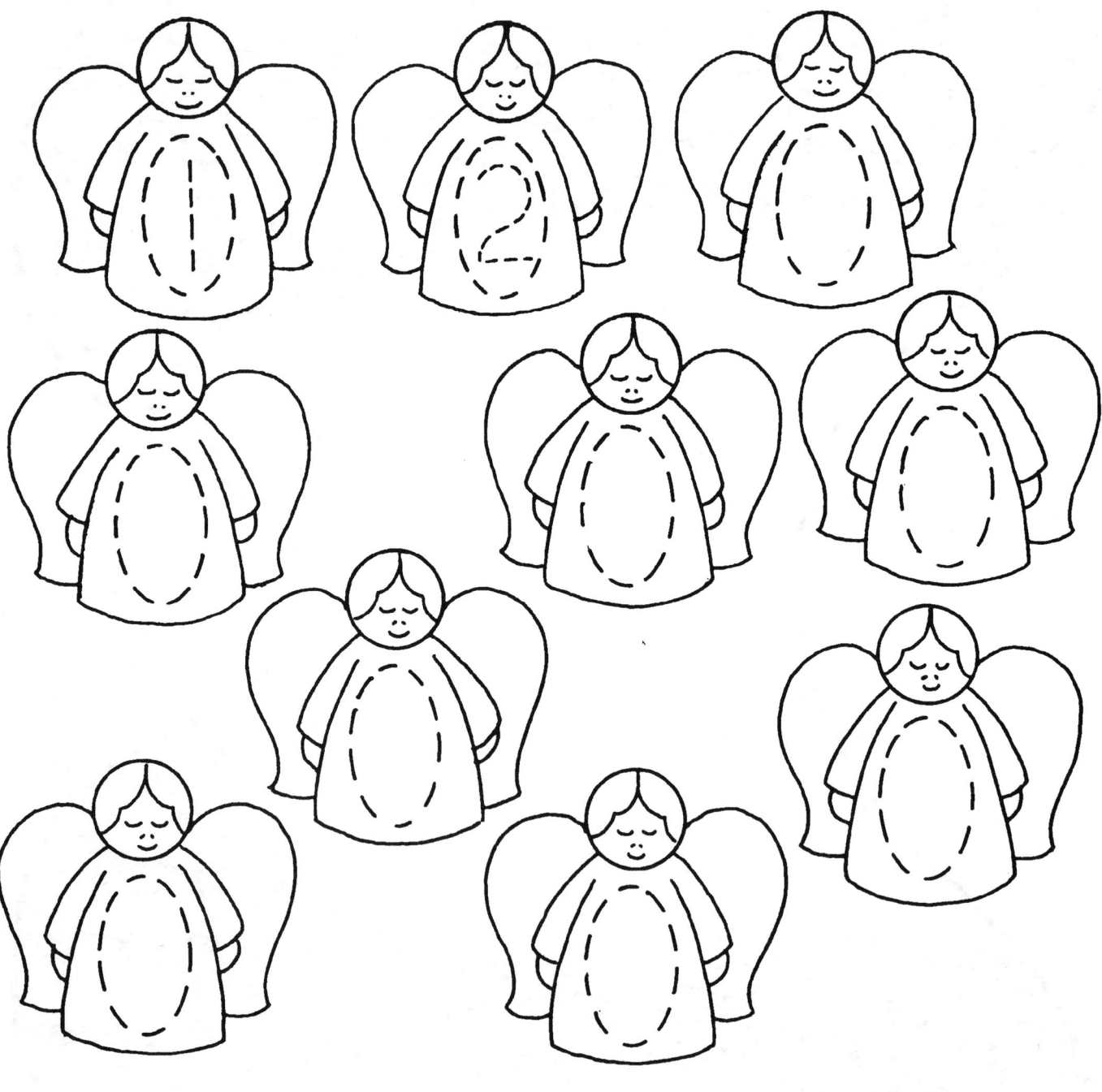

How many angels? ☐

#304 Literature Activities For Young Children, Book 5 32 © 1990 Teacher Created Materials, Inc.

Name _____

The Littlest Angel

The Angel's Special Box

1. Help the angel get his box. (There is more than one path.)
2. Color the picture.

'Twas The Night Before Christmas

By Clement C. Moore

SUMMARY

This very traditional poem describes the actions and feelings of a family anticipating the arrival of Santa Claus and his sleigh drawn by eight reindeer. The stockings are hung by the chimney and everyone goes to bed. Santa and his eight reindeer fly through the air landing on the family's rooftop. Santa goes down the chimney with his bag of toys, fills the stockings, puts toys under the tree, leaves through the chimney and flies away in his sleigh.

SUGGESTED ACTIVITIES

Christmas Gift Classification: In Christmas paper wrap many small, medium, and large boxes. Child sorts the boxes into groups by size, color, or shape.

Christmas Tree Decorating: Provide non-breakable Christmas tree decorations. Let child practice decorating a small artificial or real tree.

Christmas Presents That Belong Together: Out of old toy or educational catalogs, cut groups of pictures that belong together (teddy bears, furniture, clothes, manipulatives for building, etc.). In each group of pictures, place one that does not belong. Children find the one that does not belong and explain why the others go together.

Christmas Collage: Children cut out Christmas pictures from old Christmas cards, wrapping paper or magazines and make a collage on green or red construction paper.

Cracked Bulbs: Cut bulb shapes from construction paper. Cut each bulb in half using zig zags, curves, etc. Children will match the two halves. (Examples: upper/lower case letters, numbers/matching number of dots.)

Rhythmic Movement to Christmas Music: Children can move rhythmically to Christmas songs. Let them feel the music and bend their bodies to the music's moods and rhythms.

Name _____

'Twas the Night Before Christmas

'Twas The Night Before Christmas

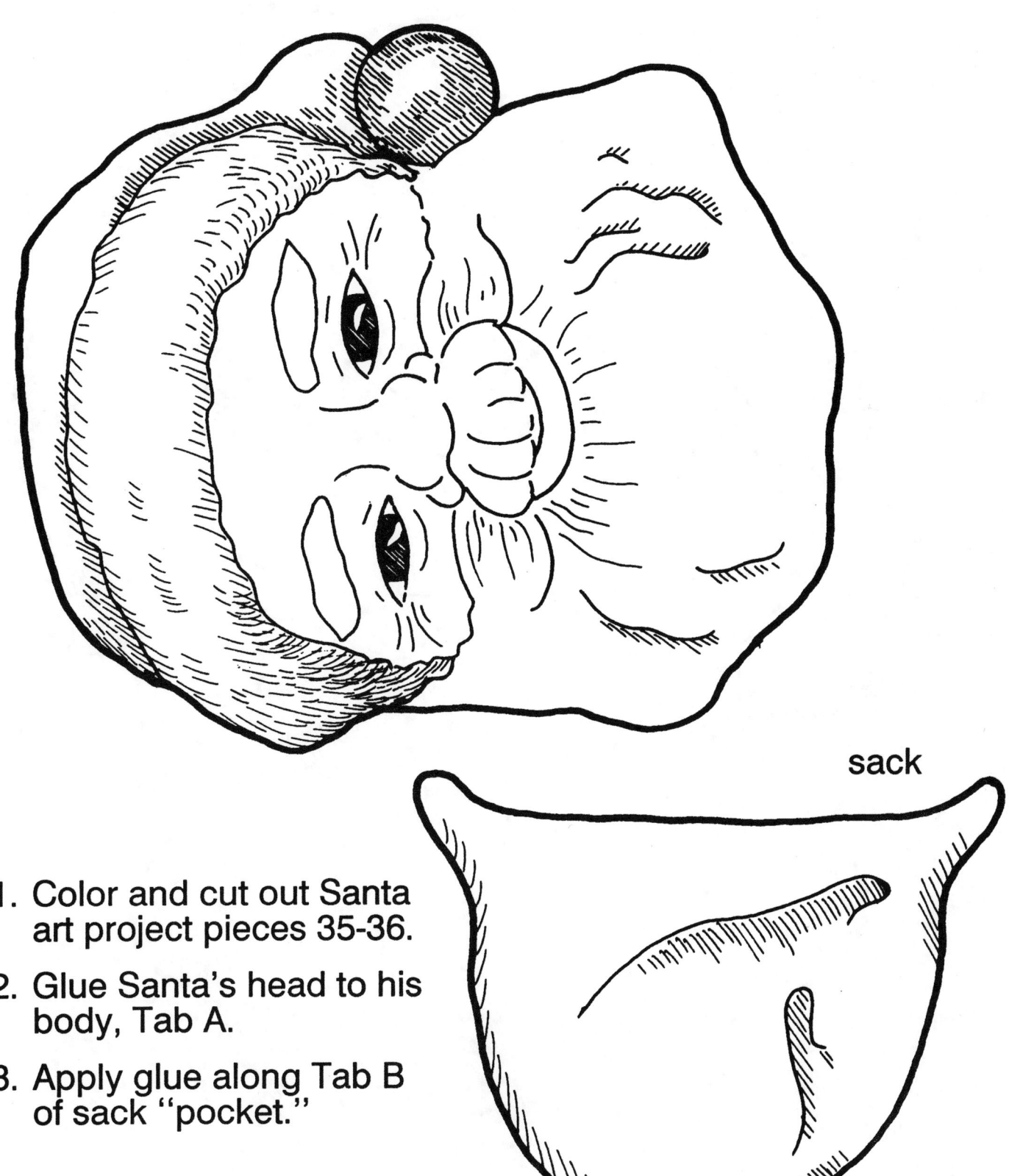

sack

1. Color and cut out Santa art project pieces 35-36.
2. Glue Santa's head to his body, Tab A.
3. Apply glue along Tab B of sack "pocket."

Name _____

'Twas the Night Before Christmas

'Twas The Night Before Christmas
(cont.)

4. Lay the "pocket" on top of Tab B.

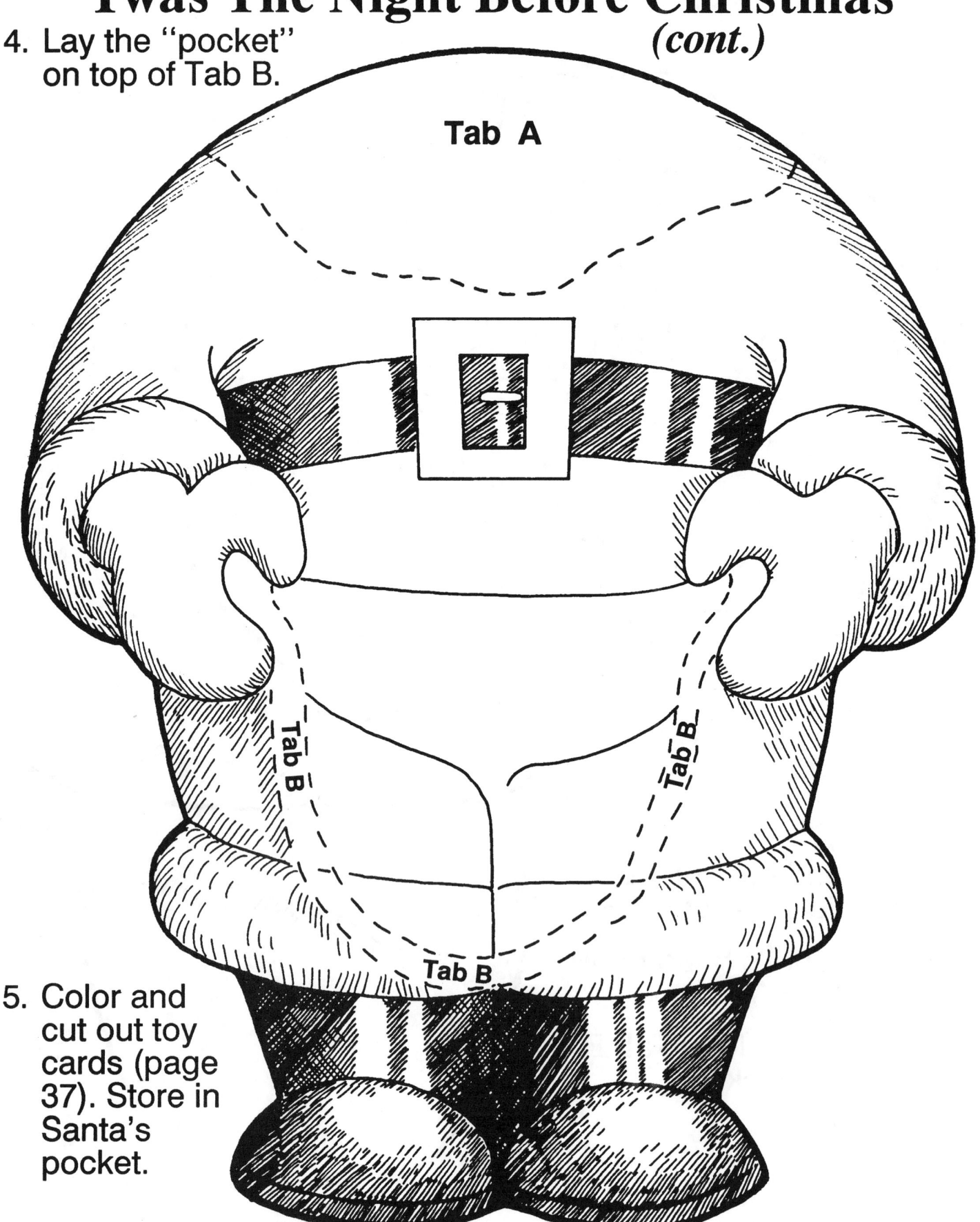

5. Color and cut out toy cards (page 37). Store in Santa's pocket.

Name _____ 'Twas the Night Before Christmas

'Twas The Night Before Christmas
(cont.)
Toy Cards

Name _____   'Twas the Night Before Christmas

Christmas Things

1. Circle and color the things in each group.

   YELLOW   things UNDER the tree
   RED   things ON the tree
   GREEN   things FOR Santa

#304 Literature Activities For Young Children, Book 5 © 1990 Teacher Created Materials, Inc.

Name _____

'Twas the Night Before Christmas

Bulbs On The Tree

1. Color the tree.
2. Color the bulbs with toys on page 40.
3. Cut out bulbs.
4. Glue onto tree.

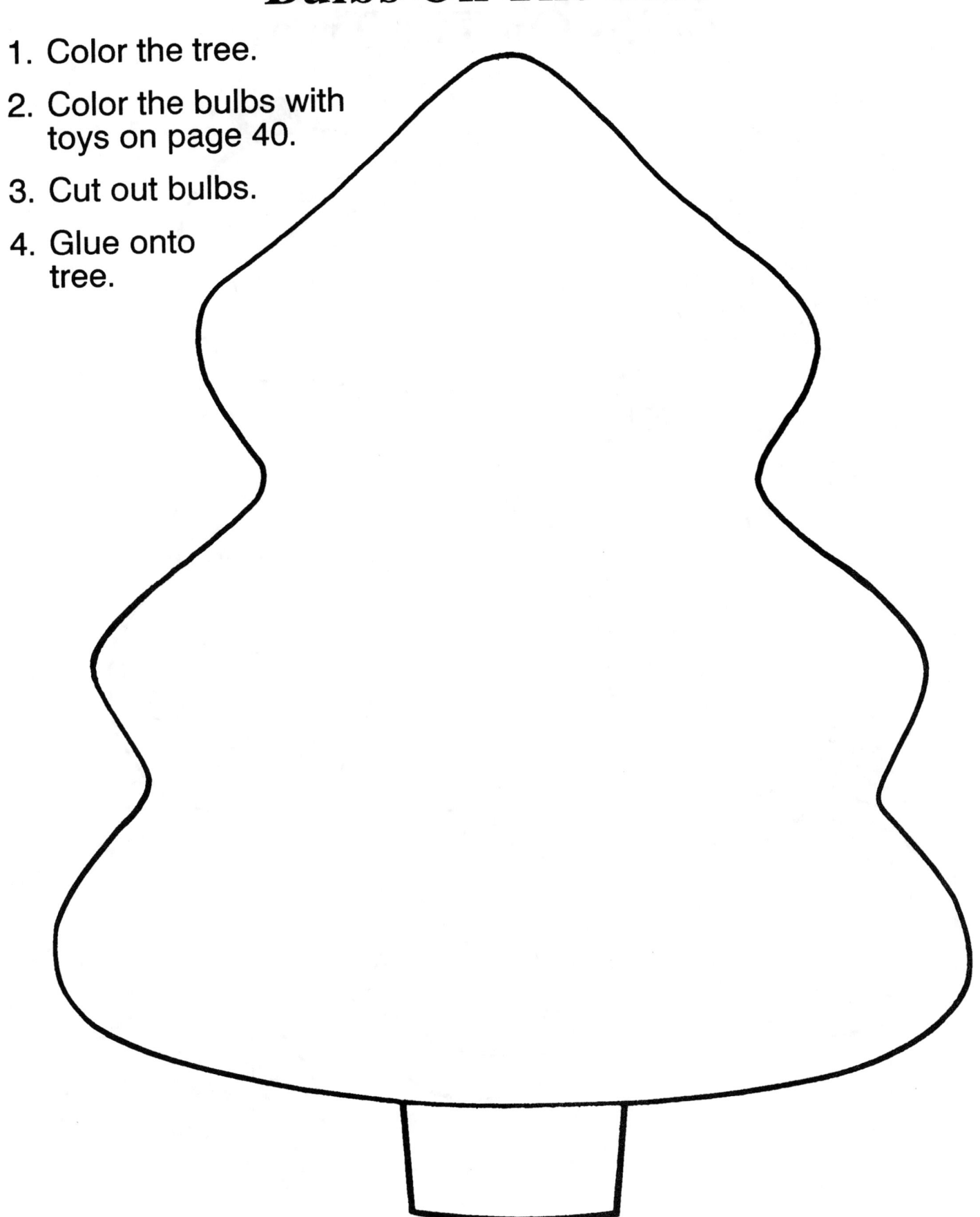

Name _____   'Twas the Night Before Christmas

Bulbs On The Tree
(cont.)

#304 Literature Activities For Young Children, Book 5 © 1990 Teacher Created Materials, Inc.

The Best Valentine In The World

By Marjorie Weinman Sharmat

SUMMARY

Ferdinand the fox spends November 5th to February 14th creating what he feels is the best valentine in the world for his girl friend, Florette. As he diligently works on his valentine during all these months, he assumes Florette is doing the same for him. February 14th finally arrives and Ferdinand makes a visit to Florette's home with his valentine. Florette has forgotten that this day is Valentine's Day. Angrily, Ferdinand leaves Florette's home, with the valentine. At his home, Ferdinand reconsiders his actions and decides to give Florette the valentine. He makes his second trip to Florette's house. To Ferdinand's surprise, Florette has made a beautiful valentine for him. Ferdinand had left before a complete explanation from Florette. Both Ferdinand and Florette enjoy their valentines.

SUGGESTED ACTIVITIES

Valentine Touching Pairs: Cut pairs of hearts out of velvet, sandpaper, satin, burlap, fake fur, etc. Have the child wear a blindfold and match the hearts.

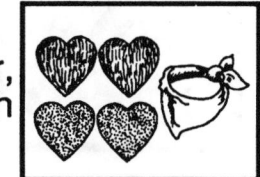

Heart Math: Give each child a large piece of paper and a box of crayons. The child writes the numbers 1-5 in a column of the left hand side of the paper. Turn the paper over, write the numbers 6-10 in a column. Child draws colored hearts in a row, next to the number.

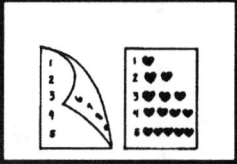

Heart Rubbing: Make some heart shapes out of sandpaper, bumpy materials, burlap, screen, etc. Place a sheet of typing paper over a heart. With the side of a peeled crayon, rub over the hearts creating patterned hearts on your paper.

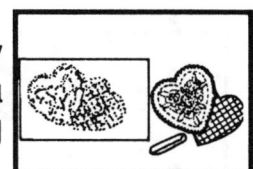

Ordinal Number Hearts: Staple two hearts together around their sides, creating pocket hearts. Print first, second, third, fourth, fifth, etc. on hearts. Children hide their eyes, teacher hides a candy heart in one of the pockets. Children take turns guessing which paper pocket heart has the candy heart.

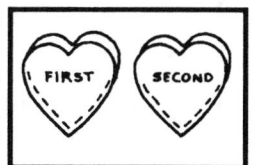

Shaving Cream Painting: Put some shaving cream on white construction paper. Sprinkle some dry tempera paint on top of shaving cream. Children mix this with their hands and finger paint a picture of some hearts. A variety of colors makes a nice display.

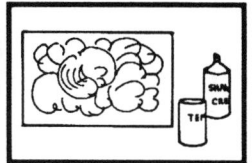

Name _____   *The Best Valentine In The World*

Pretty Valentines

1. Color and cut out the valentines.
2. Glue the valentines in order from largest to smallest.

Cut

- -

#304 Literature Activities For Young Children, Book 5 © 1990 Teacher Created Materials, Inc.

Name _____   *The Best Valentine In The World*

Valentine Shapes

1. Cut out the valentines.
2. Glue them in the correct space on page 44.
3. Color.

© 1990 Teacher Created Materials, Inc. #304 Literature Activities For Young Children, Book 5

Name _____ *The Best Valentine In The World*

Valentine Shapes
(cont.)

#304 Literature Activities For Young Children, Book 5   44   © 1990 Teacher Created Materials, Inc.

Name _____   *The Best Valentine In The World*

Pretty Valentine

1. Connect the dots.
2. Color the picture.

© 1990 Teacher Created Materials, Inc.   45   #304 Literature Activities For Young Children, Book 5

Name _____   *The Best Valentine In The World*

Decorate The Valentine

1. Cut out and color valentine and decorations (pages 46-47).
2. Cut slits in valentine.
3. Fold Tabs. Match and insert pictures into slits on valentine.

#304 Literature Activities For Young Children, Book 5

Name _____ The Best Valentine In The World

Decorate The Valentine
(cont.)

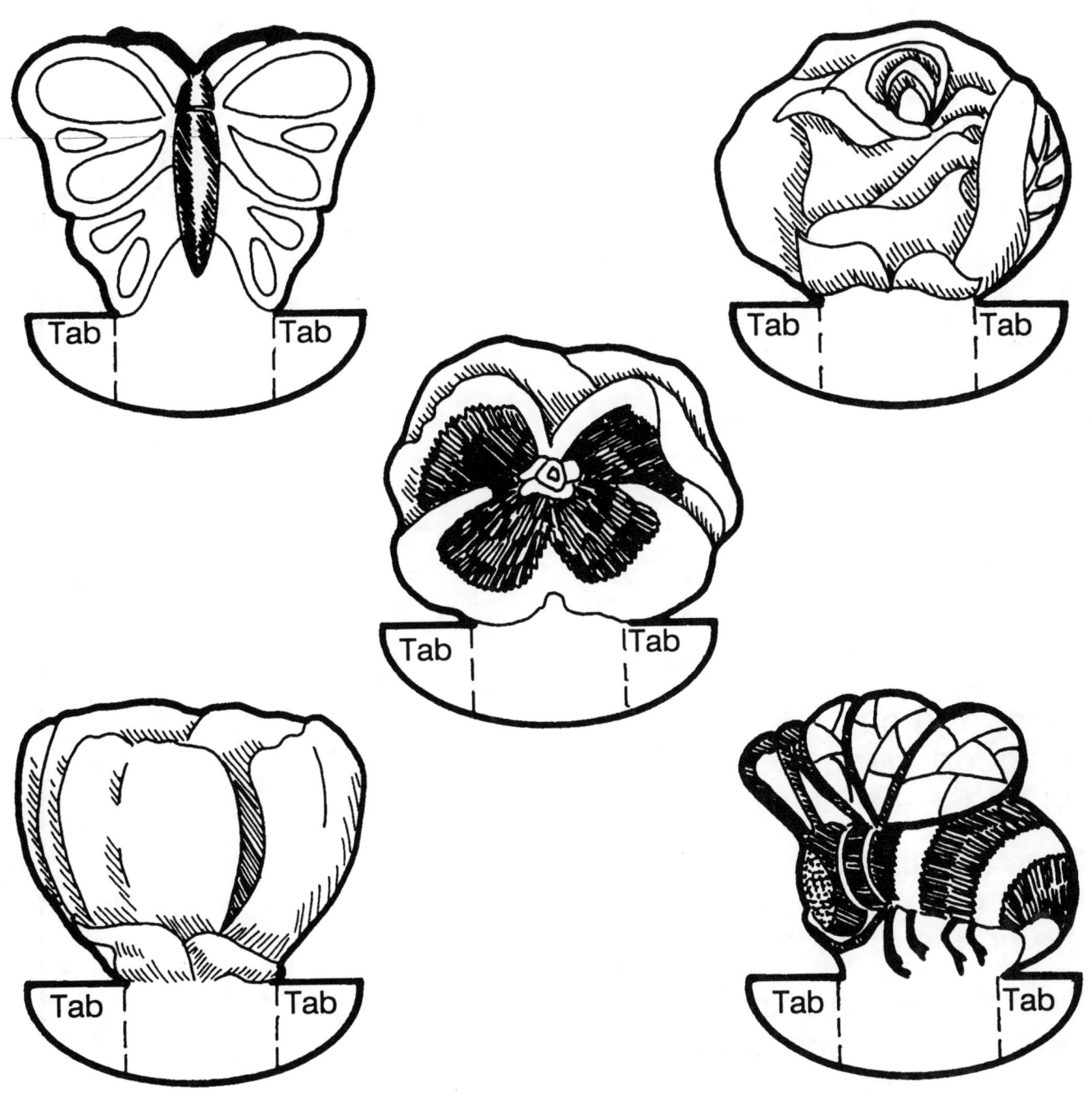

Name _____   *The Best Valentine In The World*

The Best Valentine In The World

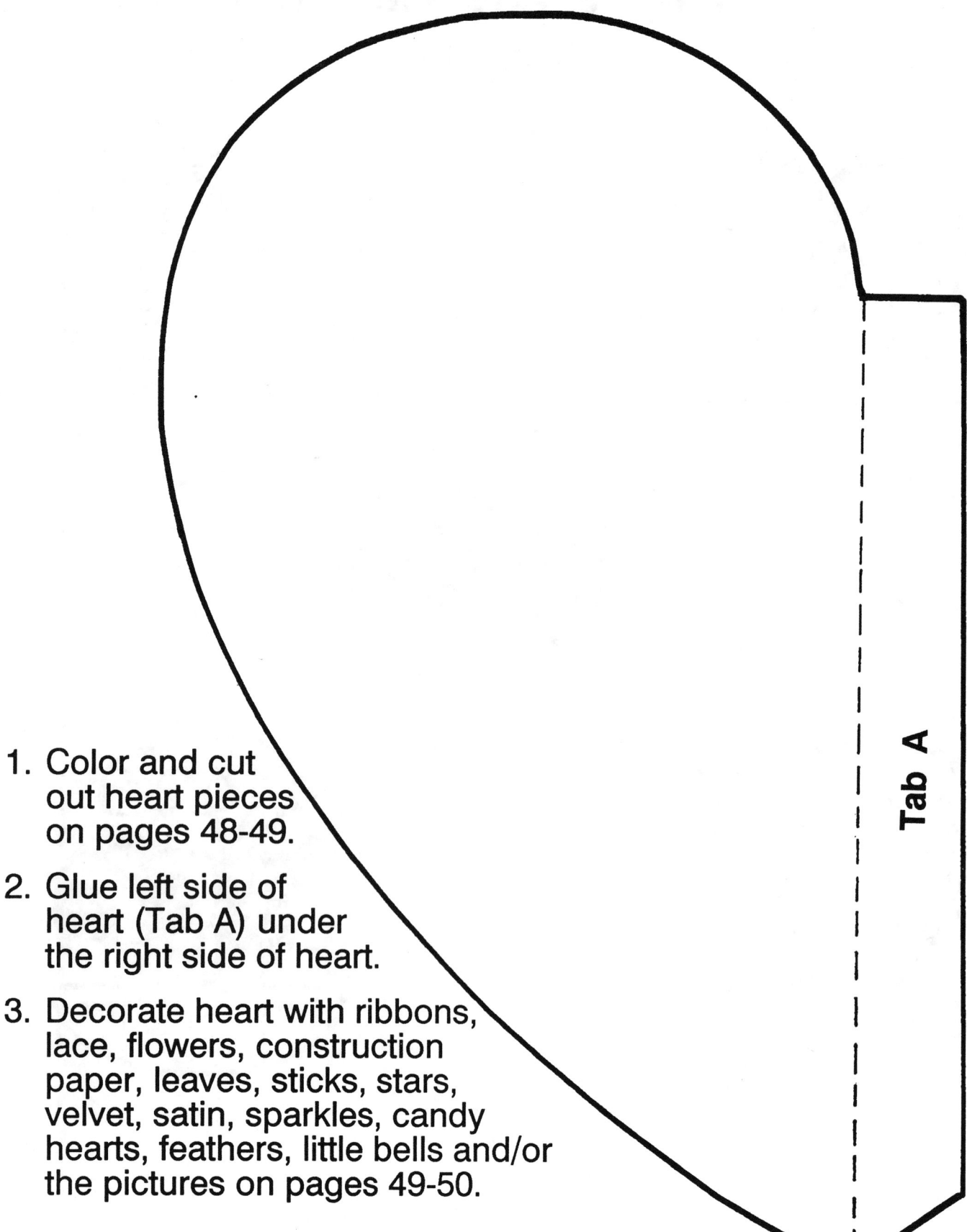

1. Color and cut out heart pieces on pages 48-49.

2. Glue left side of heart (Tab A) under the right side of heart.

3. Decorate heart with ribbons, lace, flowers, construction paper, leaves, sticks, stars, velvet, satin, sparkles, candy hearts, feathers, little bells and/or the pictures on pages 49-50.

Name _____ *The Best Valentine In The World*

The Best Valentine In The World
(cont.)

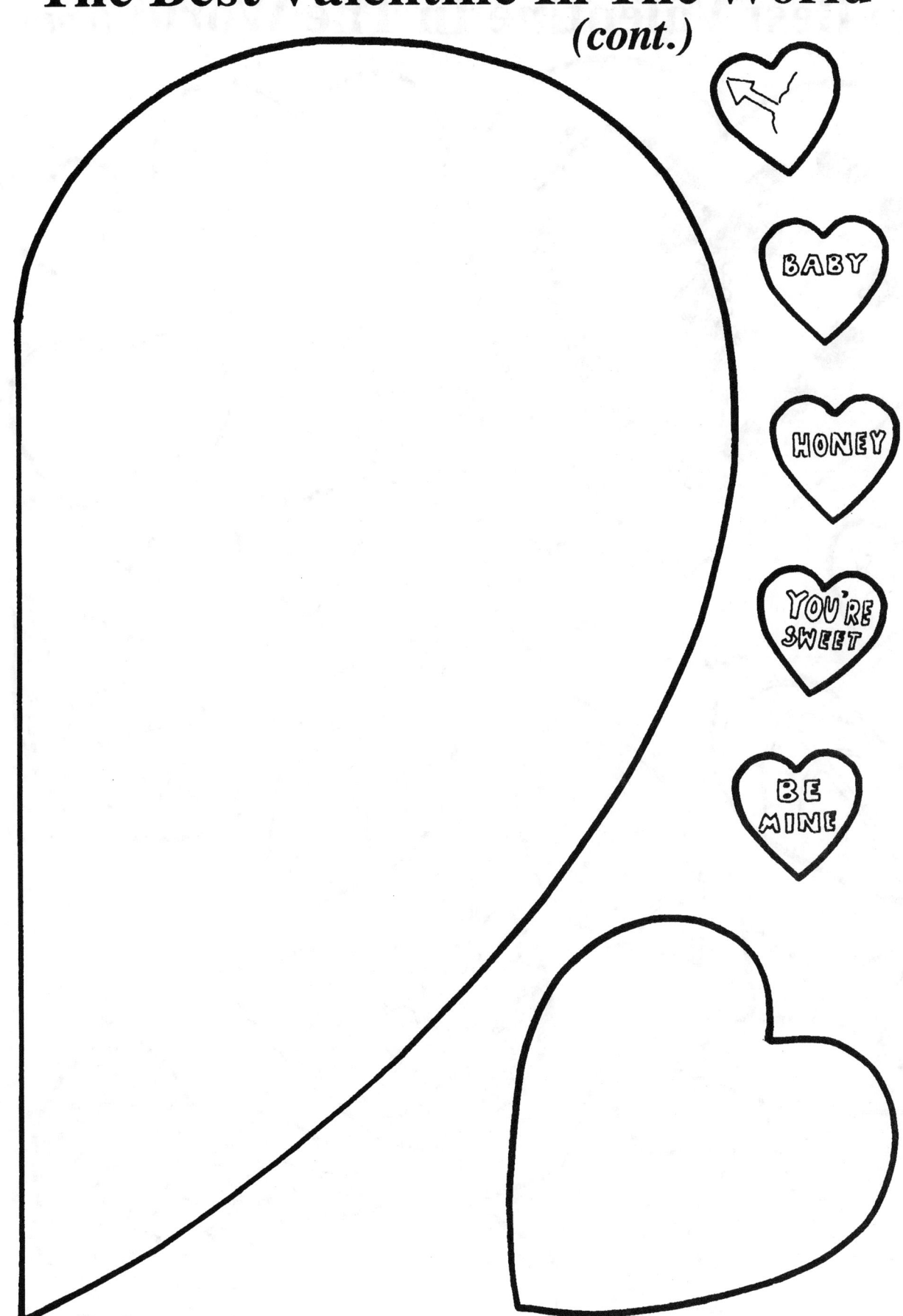

Name _____

The Best Valentine In The World

The Best Valentine In The World *(cont.)*

#304 Literature Activities For Young Children, Book 5 — 50 — © 1990 Teacher Created Materials, Inc.

The Valentine Bears

By Eve Bunting

SUMMARY

Mrs. Bear decides to celebrate Valentine's Day with her husband before the end of the hibernation, so she sets her alarm clock for February 14th. She prepares a special sign, honey, crispy critters, and two valentine poems. She wakes Mr. Bear from his deep sleep. Before hibernation, Mr. Bear has prepared some chocolate covered ants for Mrs. Bear. Both bears enjoy the holiday and then fall fast asleep again until spring.

SUGGESTED ACTIVITIES

Valentines For Bears: Color and cut out the game pieces on pages 59-61. Child matches the correct number of valentines to the number on bear's tummy.

Scrap Paper Hearts: Draw a heart on a sheet of black construction paper with chalk. Apply a thick coat of glue inside the heart shape. Tear up pieces of pink and red construction paper and attach the pieces in the heart shape.

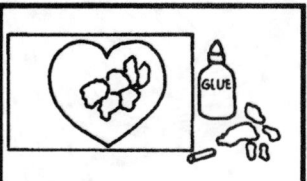

Counting Hearts: Glue one numbered heart in the bottom of each egg carton cup (1-12). Put 78 little candy hearts into the lid of the egg carton. Child counts out the appropriate number of candy hearts into each egg carton cup.

Spaghetti Painted Hearts: Cook spaghetti in boiling water until the spaghetti is wiggly. Drain and put the spaghetti in two separate bowls. Add cool water to each of the bowls. Put red food coloring in one bowl, purple food coloring in the other bowl. Draw a heart pattern onto pink construction paper. Place the spaghetti onto the pink heart in wiggles and squiggles. The starch in the spaghetti will allow the noodles to stick to the paper. Let dry.

Heart Number Book: Cut and staple 10 small sheets of paper together making a small booklet. Print numbers 1-10 on each of the pages in the book. Children glue the correct number of candy hearts to each page.

Name _____

The Valentine Bears

The Valentine Bears

1. Color and cut out bear pieces on pages 52-55.
2. Glue head onto body.
3. Attach arms and legs to body of bear at matching letters.

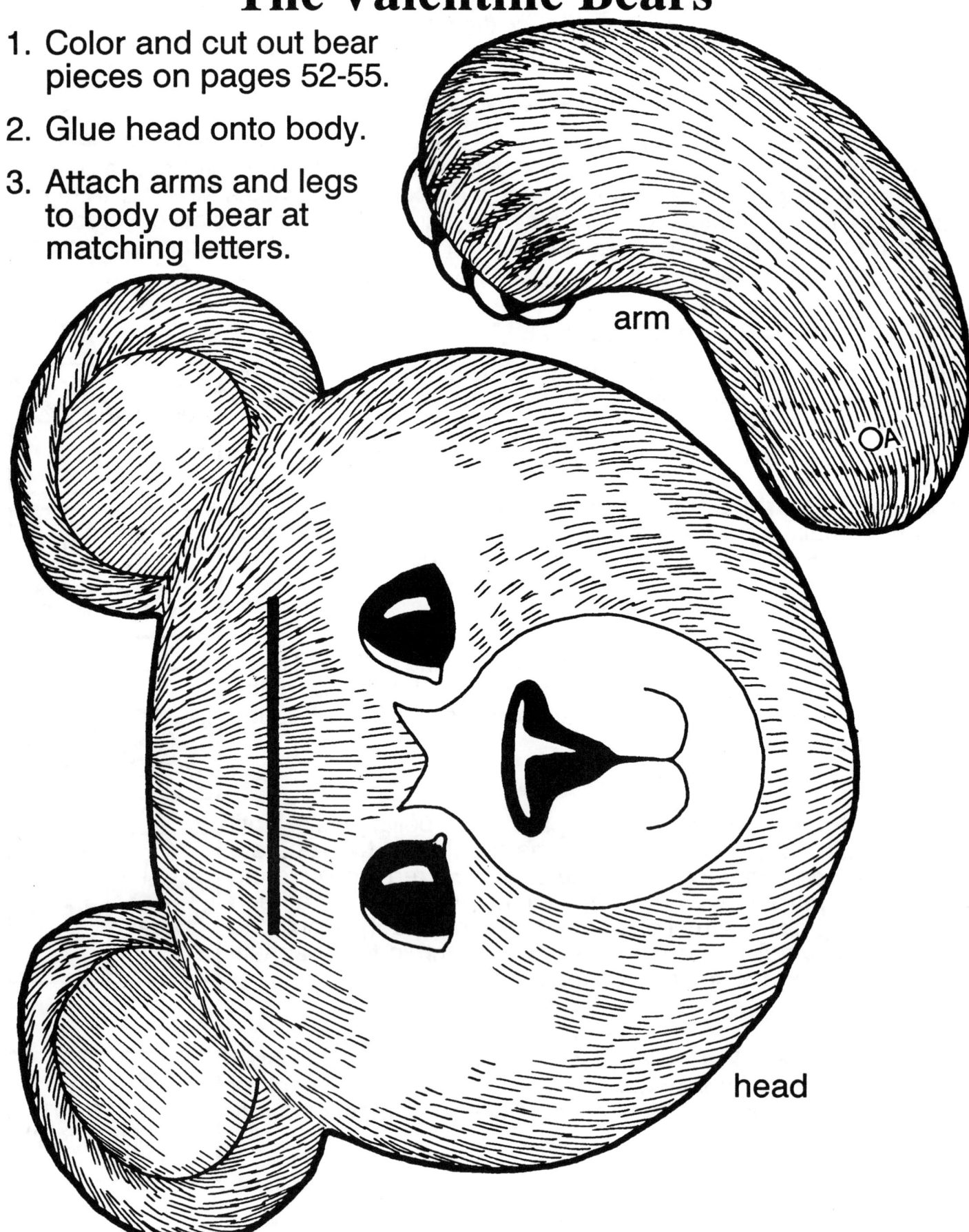

arm

head

#304 Literature Activities For Young Children, Book 5 © 1990 Teacher Created Materials, Inc.

Name _____

The Valentine Bears

The Valentine Bears
(cont.)

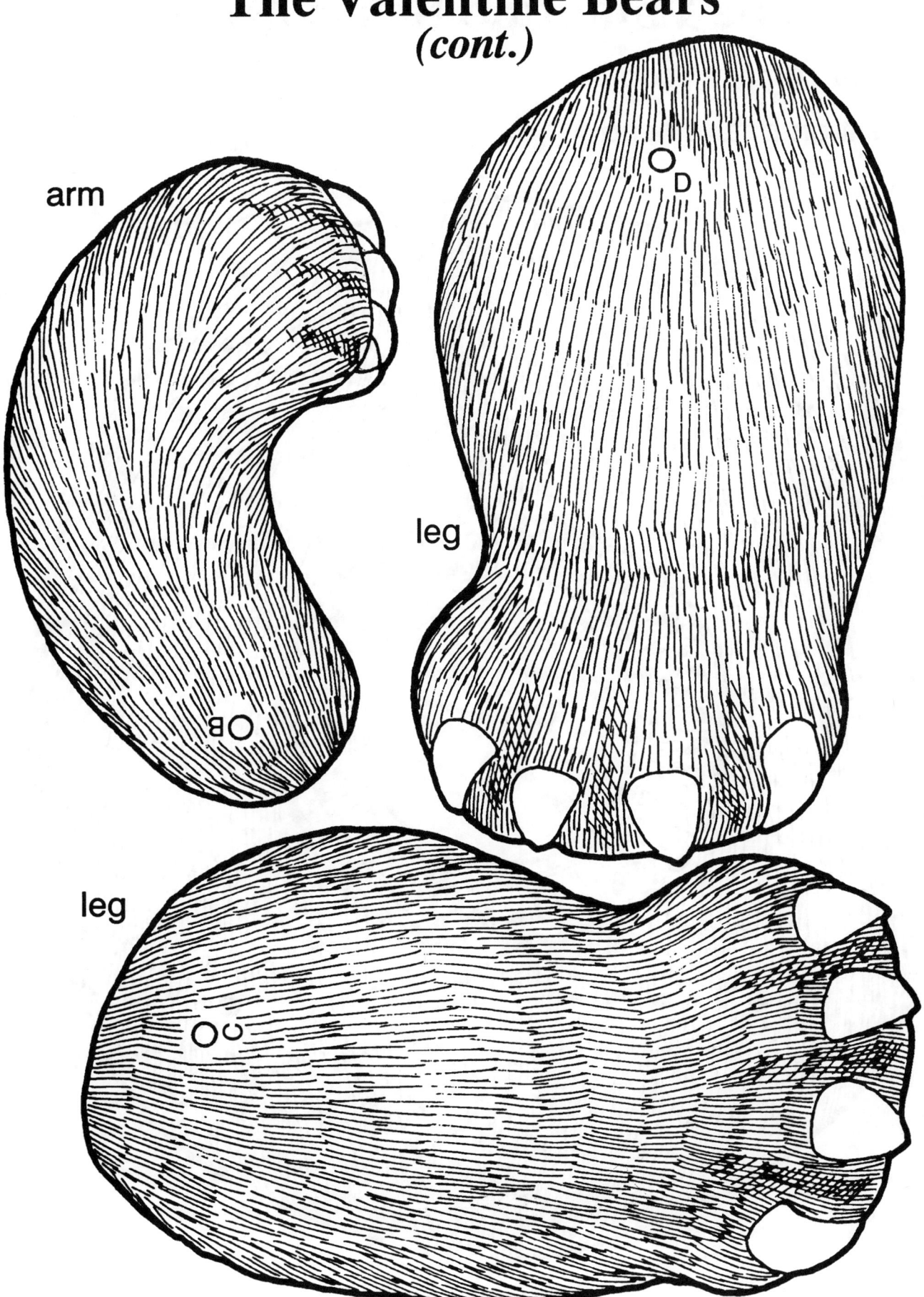

Name _____

The Valentine Bears

The Valentine Bears *(cont.)*

4. Cut out center of body.
5. Cut slit on bear's head.

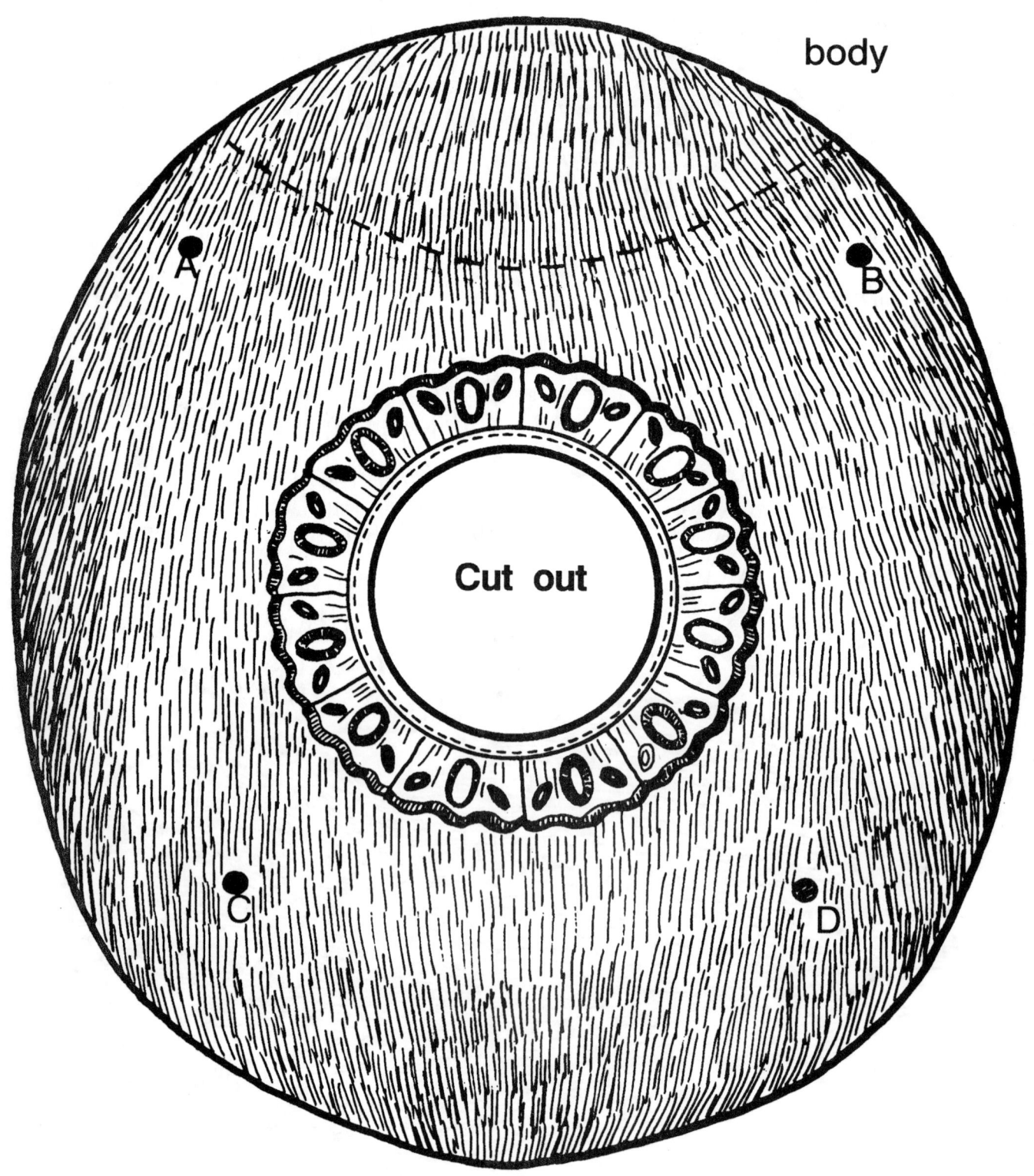

body

Cut out

#304 Literature Activities For Young Children, Book 5 — 54 — © 1990 Teacher Created Materials, Inc.

Name _____

The Valentine Bears
(cont.)

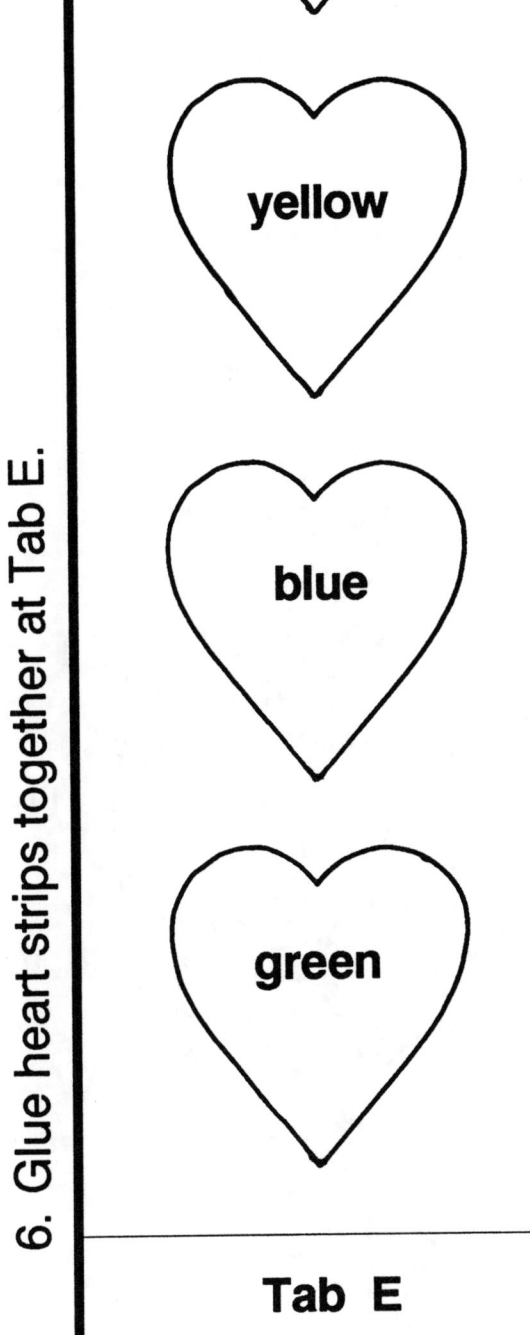

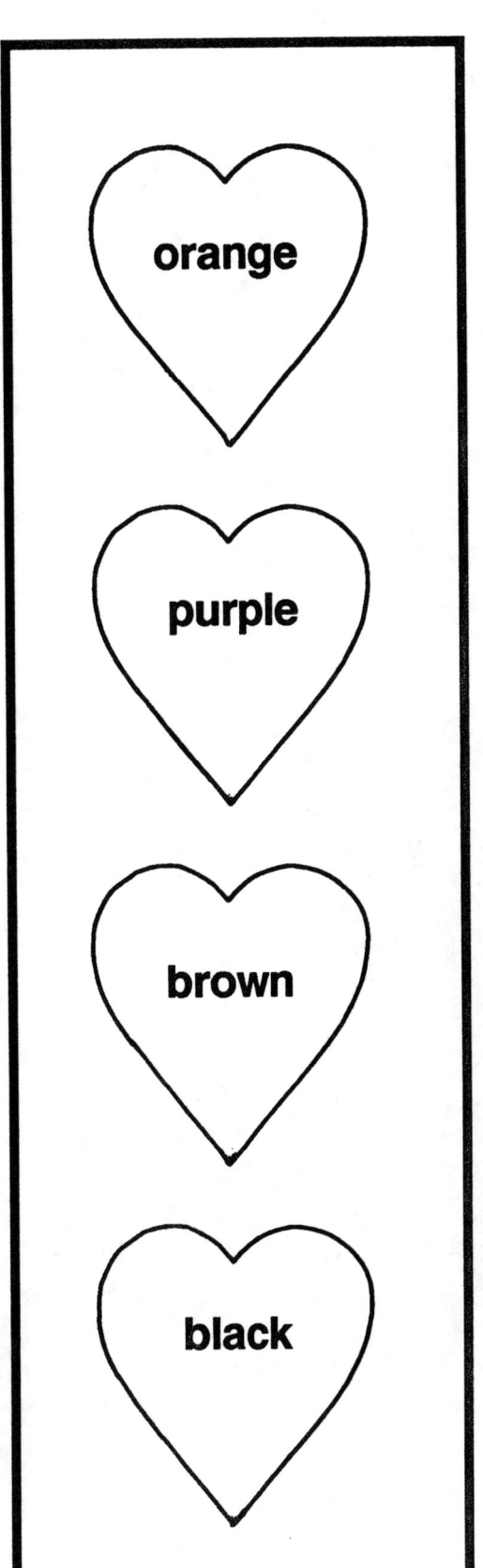

6. Glue heart strips together at Tab E.

7. Push the heart strip through the slit on the bear's head.

Name _____   *The Valentine Bears*

A Valentine Bear

1. Connect the dots.
2. Color.

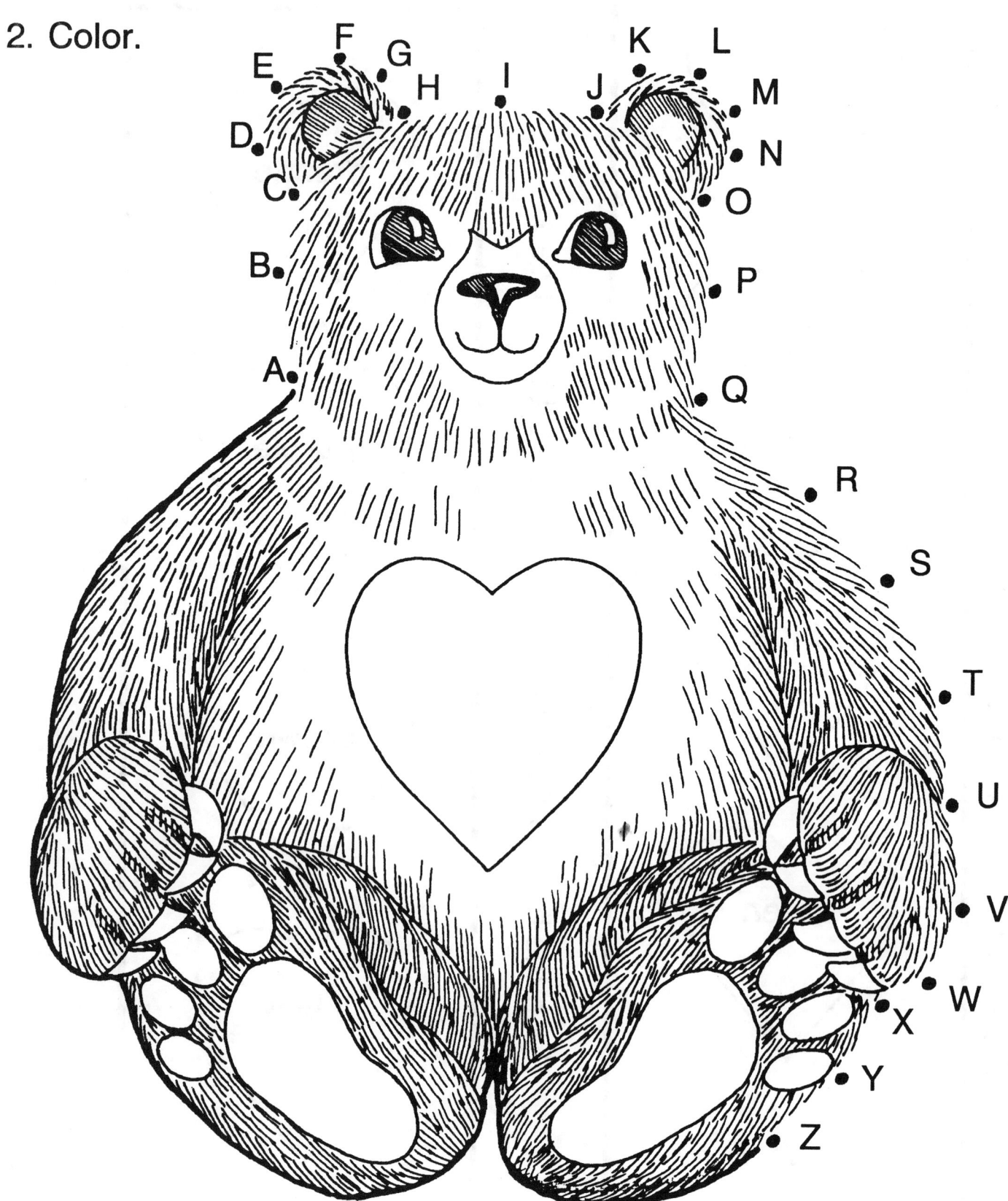

#304 Literature Activities For Young Children, Book 5 © 1990 Teacher Created Materials, Inc.

Name _____ The Valentine Bears

A Valentine For Mr. Bear

1. Find the path that helps Mrs. Bear give Mr. Bear a valentine.
2. Color.

Name _____   *The Valentine Bears*

Heart Pattern Strips

1. Cut out and glue strip pieces end to end.
2. Color the hearts in a pattern (example: red, red, blue, red, red, etc.)
3. Share your pattern with the class.

Name _____ *The Valentine Bears*

The Valentine Bears

*See suggested activity page 51.

Name _____

The Valentine Bears

The Valentine Bears *(cont.)*

*See suggested activity page 51.

Game Pieces

Name _____

The Valentine Bears

The Valentine Bears *(cont.)*

*See suggested activity page 51.

Game Pieces

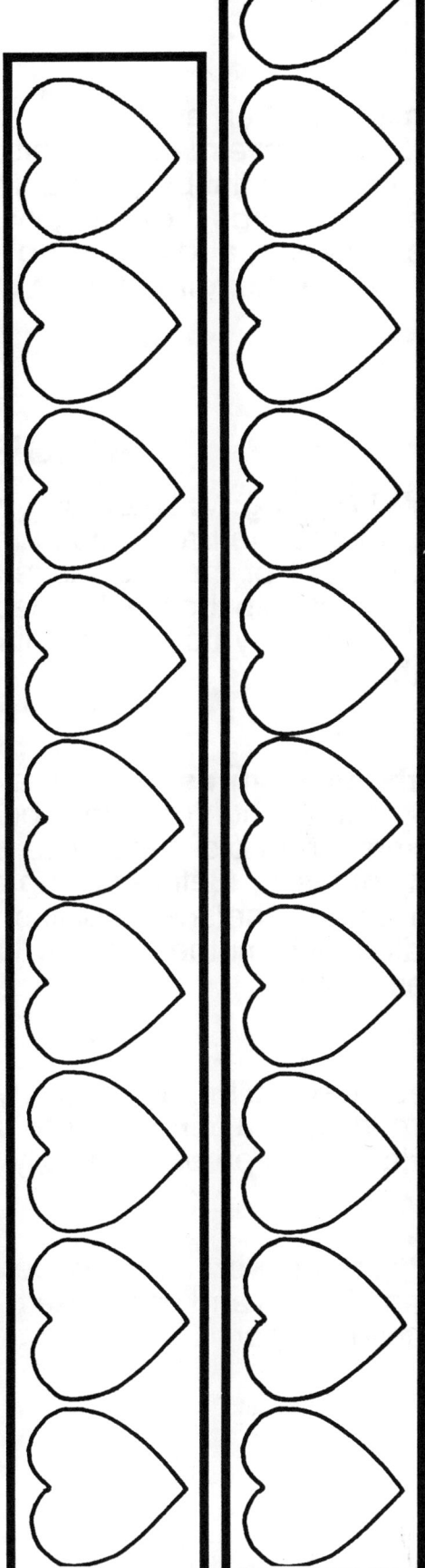

The Mother's Day Mice

by Eve Bunting

SUMMARY

Three mice children awake very early on Mother's Day and go to find gifts for their mother. They brave many dangers. Middle Mouse finds a strawberry, Biggest Mouse finds a dandelion fluffball, but Little Mouse cannot get the honeysuckle mother loves because Cat guards the cottage where it grows. He hears a piano playing inside the cottage, however, and makes up a Mother's Day poem to go with the tune. Mother Mouse loves all her gifts and the thoughtful children who brought them.

SUGGESTED ACTIVITIES

Mouse's "M" Bag: Make a fabric, drawstring bag. (A stuffed mouse holding the bag adds to the appeal of playing this game). In front of the bag place all kinds of small items. Children must help the teacher decide which items to put in the "m" bag. Only items beginning with the letter "m" go inside the bag.

Motherhood Pictures: Cut out a picture of a mother and staple it to the center of a small bulletin board. Children cut out pictures from old magazines of women/mothers doing a variety of tasks. Before putting the child's picture on the bulletin board, he/she explains why his/her picture is associated with mothers today. Label your bulletin board "Mothers Today."

Scented Flowers: Provide a variety of liquid tempera paints. Add lemon, vanilla, cinnamon or peppermint extract to the paint. Have children paint "smelly" flowers for mother.

Torn Paper Flowers: Tear paper into flower petals. Tear stems and leaves and add these to the petals. Glue to white construction paper.

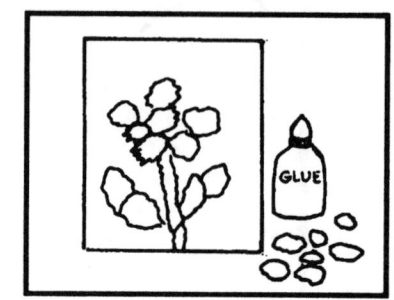

Name _____

The Mother's Day Mice

Mother's Day Mice

1. Color and cut out mouse on pages 63-64.

2. Glue the mouse's head to body, Tab A, page 64.

3. Cut and color the "Things to Do for Mother" booklet (pages 65 and 66).

4. Glue the stapled booklet onto the mouse's body.

Name _____ The Mother's Day Mice

Mother's Day Mice
(cont.)

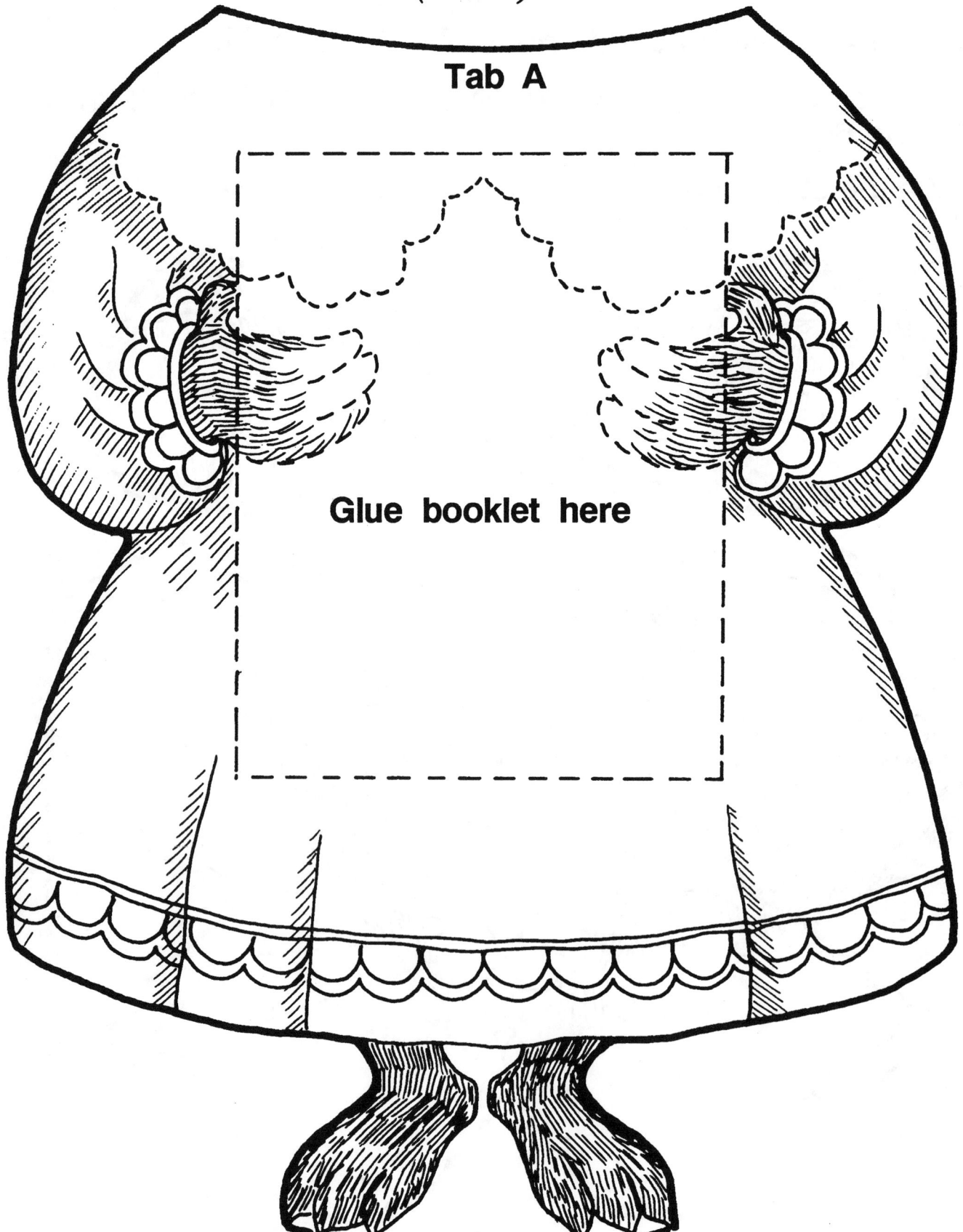

Tab A

Glue booklet here

Name _____ The Mother's Day Mice

Mother's Day Mice
(cont.)

Name _____

The Mother's Day Mice

Mother's Day Mice
(cont.)

#304 Literature Activities For Young Children, Book 5   66   © 1990 Teacher Created Materials, Inc.

Name _____   *The Mother's Day Mice*

Mother's Day Present

1. Help the mice give a present to their mother.
2. Color the pictures.

Name _____   *The Mother's Day Mice*

A Gift For Mother

1. Color, cut out, and glue the things that mothers like to get as presents.
2. Color.

#304 Literature Activities For Young Children, Book 5 — 68 — © 1990 Teacher Created Materials, Inc.

Name _____   The Mother's Day Mice

Mice in Order

1. Color and cut out the mice.
2. Glue the pieces in order from youngest to oldest.

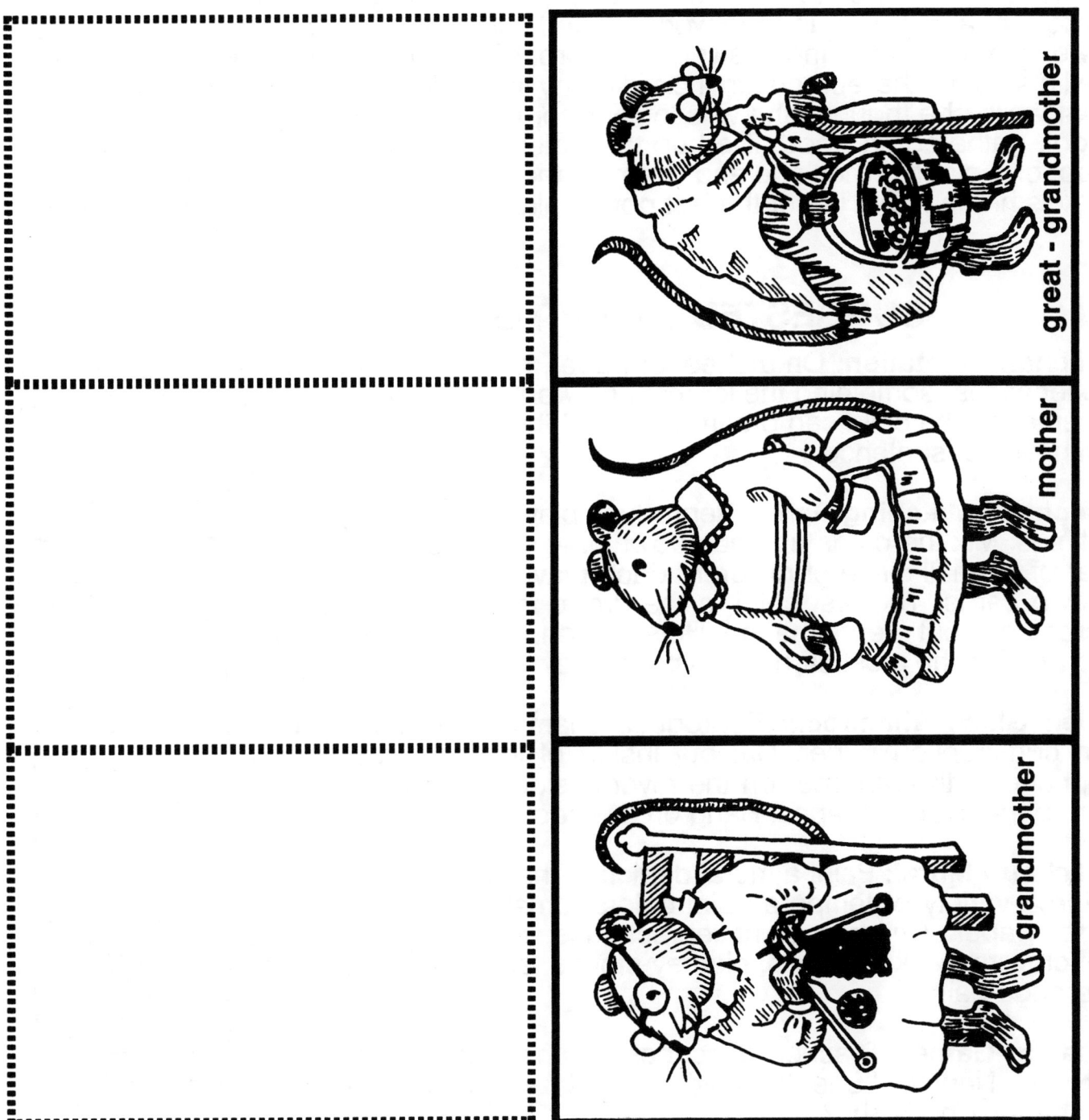

Leprechauns Never Lie

By Lorna Balian

SUMMARY

Ninny Nanny and Gram lived in a little thatched hut. The thatched roof needed patching, the potatoes needed to be dug, the firewood needed to be gathered, and the water barrel needed to be filled. But Ninny was too lazy to do the work and Gram was old and ailing. The undone work created a leaking roof and near starvation for the two. Ninny decided the answer to her problems was to catch a leprechaun and find all his gold. The leprechaun tricked Ninny into doing all the needed work around the hut while she thought she was looking for the leprechaun's gold. She thatched the roof, gathered firewood, filled up the water barrel, and dug up all her potatoes (except one plant). Then she and Gram let the leprechaun go free. The leprechaun found his hidden gold under the last potato plant and left to hide it in a safer place.

SUGGESTED ACTIVITIES

Leprechaun Dictation: On a sheet of paper, have the child dictate (teacher writes) something the leprechaun would say. This could be any sentence the child can dream up. Child then draws a picture to go with his/her sentence.

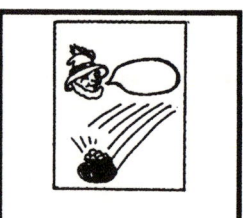

Leprechaun Matching Game: Reproduce playing cards on page 76 four times. Mix the cards up, face down. Lay the cards down in the center of a small circle of children. Each player takes turns turning over two cards. The first child in the group to spot two matching pictures calls out "leprechaun." He/she then keeps the two cards. The child with the most cards wins the game.

Stained Glass Shamrock: Reproduce shamrock (page 77) onto green construction paper. Cut out inside of leaves. Glue orange cellophane or tissue paper on the reverse side of the shamrock to cover up the cut out shapes. Hang on a window.

Leprechaun Mural: Paint a mural depicting the life of a leprechaun. Provide a variety of tempera paint colors, brushes, a large strip of butcher paper. Children paint leprechauns, mushrooms, castles, 4-leaf clovers, walking sticks, blarney stones, etc. Use lots of green and orange paint.

Guessing Game: Teacher describes a character in the story; e.g., Ninny Nanny—"She is a little girl, lazy, wants to catch a leprechaun. Who is she?"

Name _____   *Leprechauns Never Lie*

Leprechauns Never Lie

1. Color and cut out leprechaun pieces on pages 71-73.
2. Glue head onto body, Tab A.
3. Cut out space on body.

Name _____   *Leprechauns Never Lie*

Leprechauns Never Lie *(cont.)*

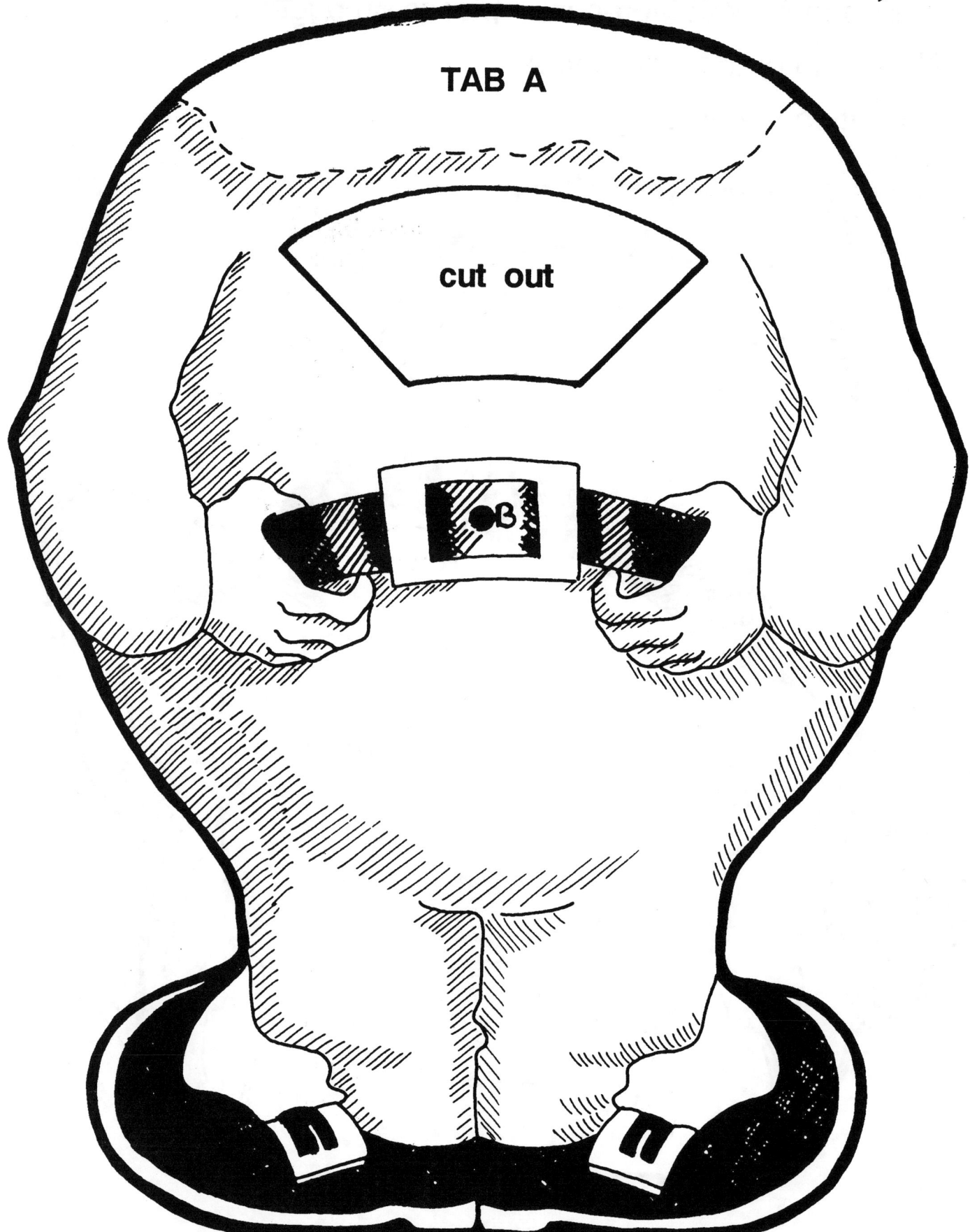

Name _____   *Leprechauns Never Lie*

Leprechauns Never Lie
(cont.)

4. Attach the wheel behind the body with a paper fastener through holes B. Turn the wheel to show the pictures through the cut out space.

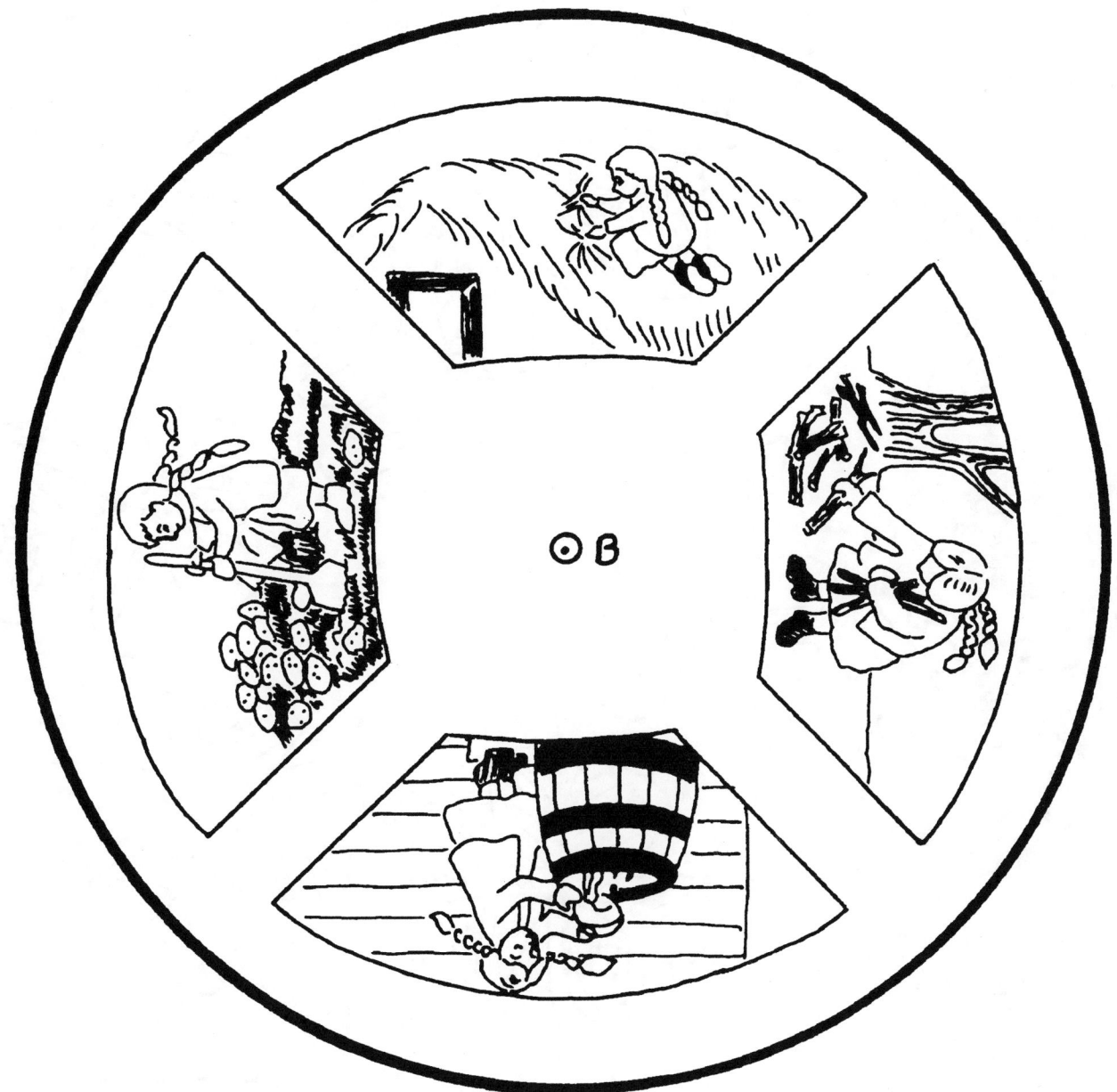

© 1990 Teacher Created Materials, Inc.

Name _____   *Leprechauns Never Lie*

How Many Shamrocks?

1. Count the shamrocks.
2. Write the answer.
3. Color.

How many shamrocks? ☐

Name _____   Leprechauns Never Lie

Ninny Nanny, Gram, Leprechaun

1. Color, cut and glue to complete the characters.

© 1990 Teacher Created Materials, Inc.   75   #304 Literature Activities For Young Children, Book 5

Name _____   *Leprechauns Never Lie*

Leprechaun Card Game

*See suggested activity page 70.

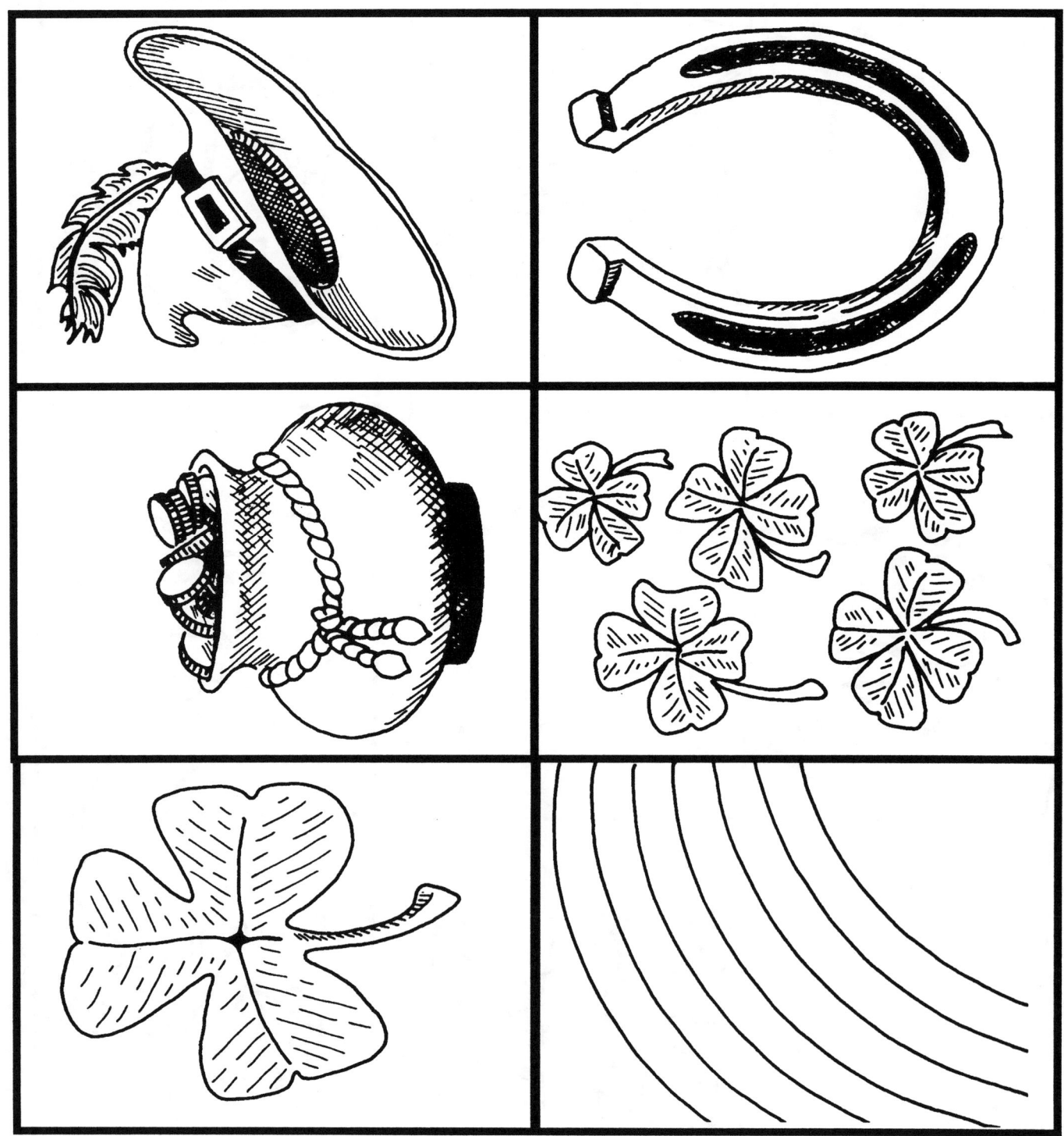

Name _____   *Leprechauns Never Lie*

Leprechauns Never Lie

*See suggested activity page 70.

Home For A Bunny

By Margaret Wise Brown

SUMMARY

A little bunny goes down a woodsy path looking for a home. He discovers the bird family has a home in a nest in a tree, the frog has a home in the bog, the groundhog has a home in a log. He meets another bunny who has a home under the ground. This bunny invites the little bunny into his home. This home becomes the little bunny's home.

SUGGESTED ACTIVITIES

Bunny Lacing Card: Reproduce the bunny pattern (page 84) onto tagboard. Punch out the holes. Cut long length of yarn, attach tape to the ends of the yarn piece. Child uses the yarn to lace the bunny.

Bunny Sack Puppet: Glue the bunny head and body (patterns on pages 85 and 86) onto a small paper bag.

Bunny Costumes: Ears: Cut a strip of pink construction paper to make a headband. Cut out two ear shapes. Color the inner ear pink or make it out of pink construction paper. Attach ears to headband. Optional: Make boy bunny ears—black headband, black outer ears with pink inner ears. Tails: Wrap white yarn many times around the width of a small book. Remove the yarn from book. Tie another piece of yarn around center of yarn loop. Clip the ends. With a safety pin, attach the tails to the child's backside. Noses and Whiskers: Put red lipstick on children's noses and use brown eyebrow pencils to draw on whiskers. Let the children hop around and pretend to be bunnies in their costumes.

Dramatic Play: Characters: 2 bunnies, 1 groundhog, 1 bird and 3 baby birds, 1 frog. Children can act out the simple progression of this story.

Tap, Clap, Snap Your Fingers, Stomp Your Feet To Songs: Children enjoy tapping a tabletop or book with a pencil or stick, snapping their fingers, clapping their hands, stomping their feet to the beat and rhythm of Easter and bunny songs.

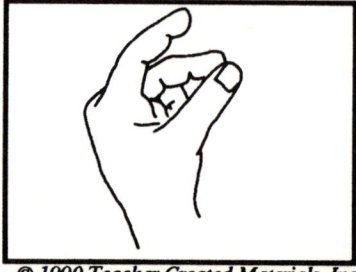

Name _____

Home For A Bunny

Home For A Bunny

1. Color and cut out the bunny art project pieces on pages 79-80.

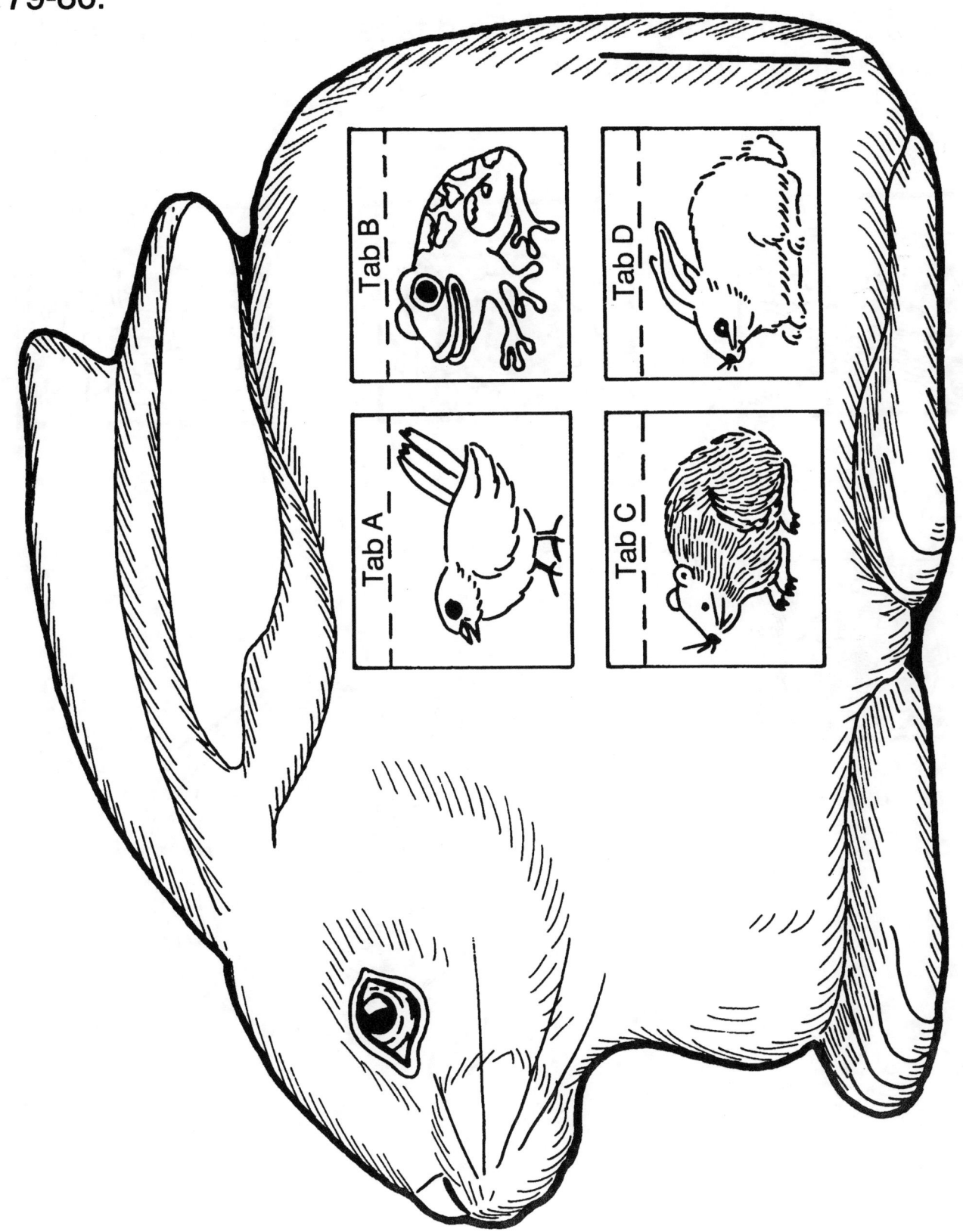

© 1990 Teacher Created Materials, Inc.   79   #304 Literature Activities For Young Children, Book 5

Name _____   Home For A Bunny

Home For A Bunny *(cont.)*

2. Attach flaps (A-D) on top of tabs A-D.
3. Tail: Cut slit in bunny's body. Fold tabs E and F downward. Insert tail into slit on bunny.

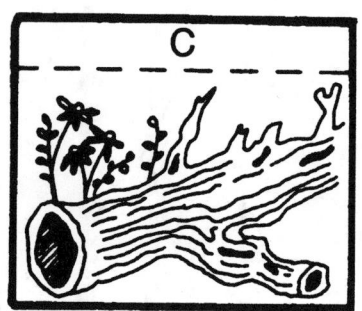
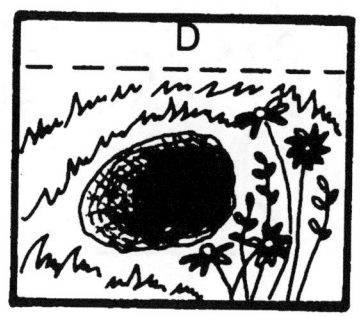

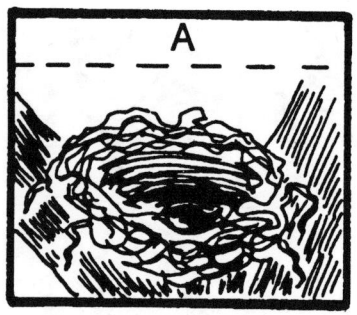
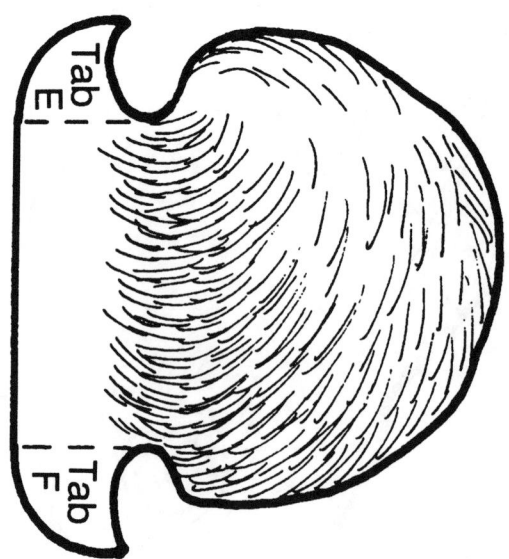

Name _____   *Home For A Bunny*

Animal Homes

1. Draw a home for each animal.
2. Color.

© 1990 Teacher Created Materials, Inc.   #304 Literature Activities For Young Children, Book 5

Name _____   Home For A Bunny

Bunny Letters

Color the bunny in each row whose letter is different.

Name _____

Home For A Bunny

Story Sequence

1. Color the pictures.
2. Cut and glue in order.

A

B

C

D

© 1990 Teacher Created Materials, Inc. 83 #304 Literature Activities For Young Children, Book 5

Name _____ Home For A Bunny

Bunny Lacing Card

*See suggested activity page 78.

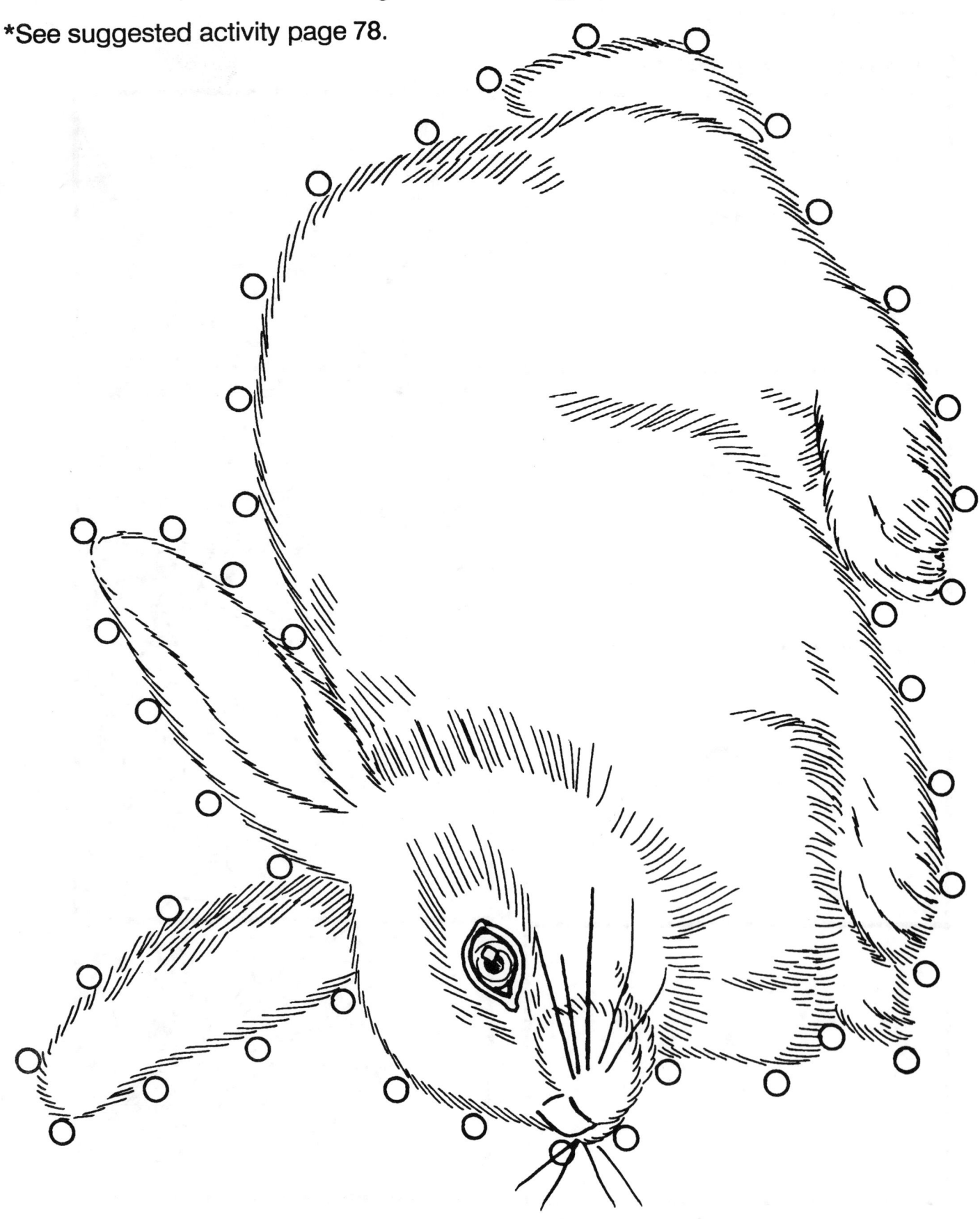

#304 Literature Activities For Young Children, Book 5   84   © 1990 Teacher Created Materials, Inc.

Name _____   Home For A Bunny

Paper Bag Bunny

*See suggested activity page 78.

© 1990 Teacher Created Materials, Inc.   #304 Literature Activities For Young Children, Book 5

Name _____

Home For A Bunny

Paper Bag Bunny
(cont.)

*See suggested activity page 78.

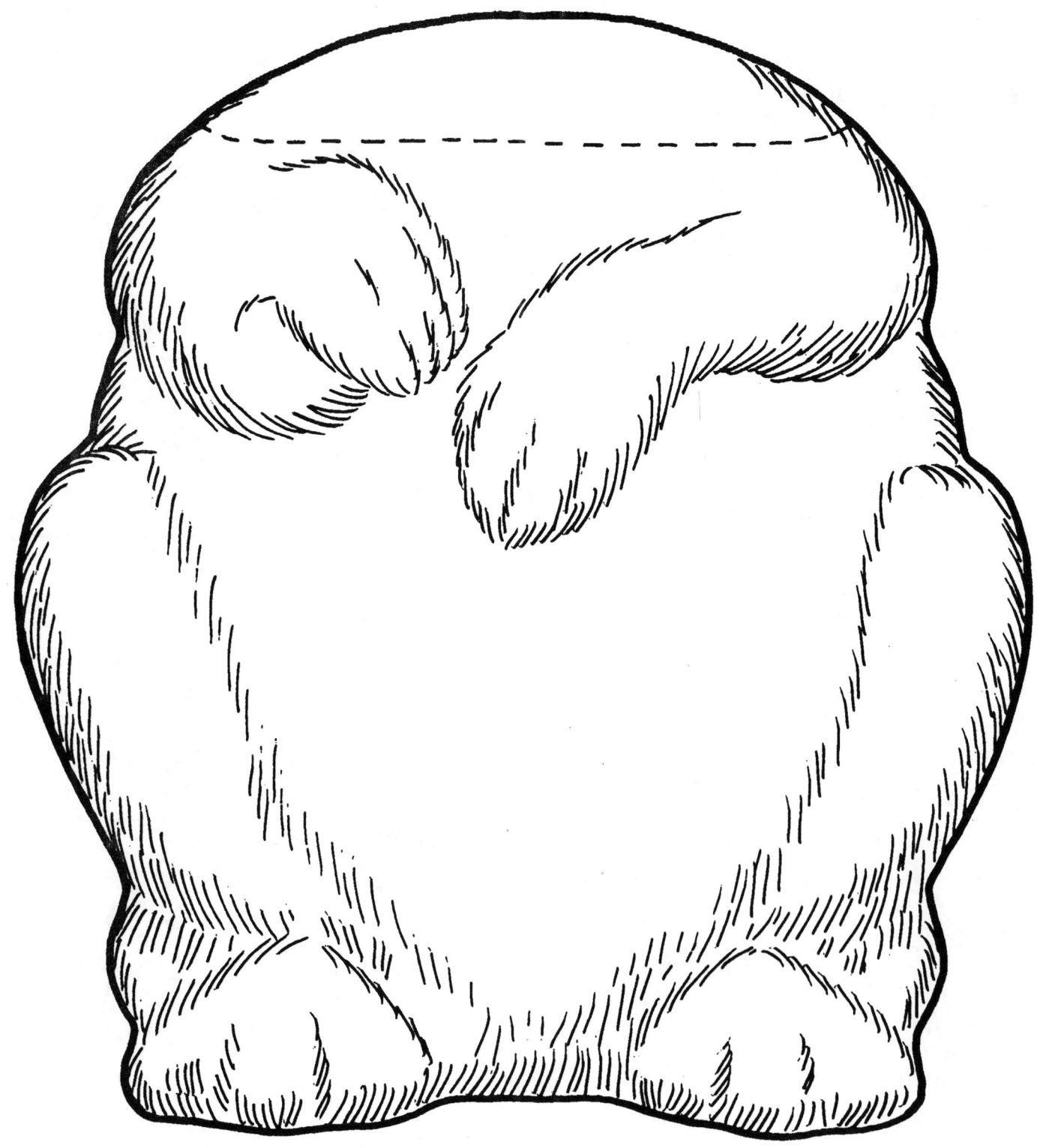

The Country Bunny And The Little Gold Shoes

By Du Bose Heyward

Summary

A little girl bunny hopes to grow up to be one of the five chosen Easter Bunnies to deliver eggs to boys and girls all over the world on Easter Eve. When she grows up and has a family of 21 babies, it seems to be the end of her dream. However, the bunny is chosen because of her qualities of being wise (she had trained all 21 baby bunnies to do the work needed to run a home), kind (she had a happy home), and swift (she had practice keeping all 21 bunnies together). On Easter Eve she delivers all her eggs except one special egg for a sick little boy living at the top of a mountain. The little rabbit goes through tremendous hardships trying to deliver the egg, but fails to get up the mountain. Grandfather Bunny, impressed with her bravery, gives her a pair of magical gold shoes. She flies up the mountain and delivers the egg. The bunny finally arrives home to her 21 babies, bringing them a basket of Easter eggs.

SUGGESTED ACTIVITIES

Bunny Shirts and Shorts: Cut two bunnies (pattern on page 95) out of yellow tagboard. Cut shirts and shorts (patterns on page 95) out of patterned wallpaper. Children find matching shirt and short sets to dress the bunnies.

Bunny Measurement: Have the children line up their toy bunnies according to height - tallest to shortest and vice versa.

Spatter Paint Bunny: Cut a rectangle out of a plastic lid. Leave a border around the lid. Put a wire screen over the lid opening. With strapping tape, secure the wire screen over the lid opening. Reproduce the bunny shape (page 96) onto white construction paper. Place bunny shape under the lid. Dip a toothbrush into some thinned tempera paint and brush over the screen. Move screen and change colors to make a colorful speckled bunny!

Marshmallow Bunnies: With round toothpicks connect two big marshmallows (body). Attach little marshmallows for ears and tail. Attach raisins for eyes and buttons.

Bunny Sand-Casting: Wet some sand with water. Make a simple bunny imprint in the sand. Mix up some plaster of Paris and pour into the bunny mold. Let plaster of Paris dry and then remove.

Name_____   The Country Bunny and The Little Gold Shoes

The Country Bunny

1. Color and cut out bunny pieces pages 88-91.

#304 Literature Activities For Young Children, Book 5   88   © 1990 Teacher Created Materials, Inc.

Name _____ *The Country Bunny and The Little Gold Shoes*

The Country Bunny *(cont.)*

2. Glue top of bunny to bottom of bunny, Tab A.
3. Put glue along edge B of pocket.

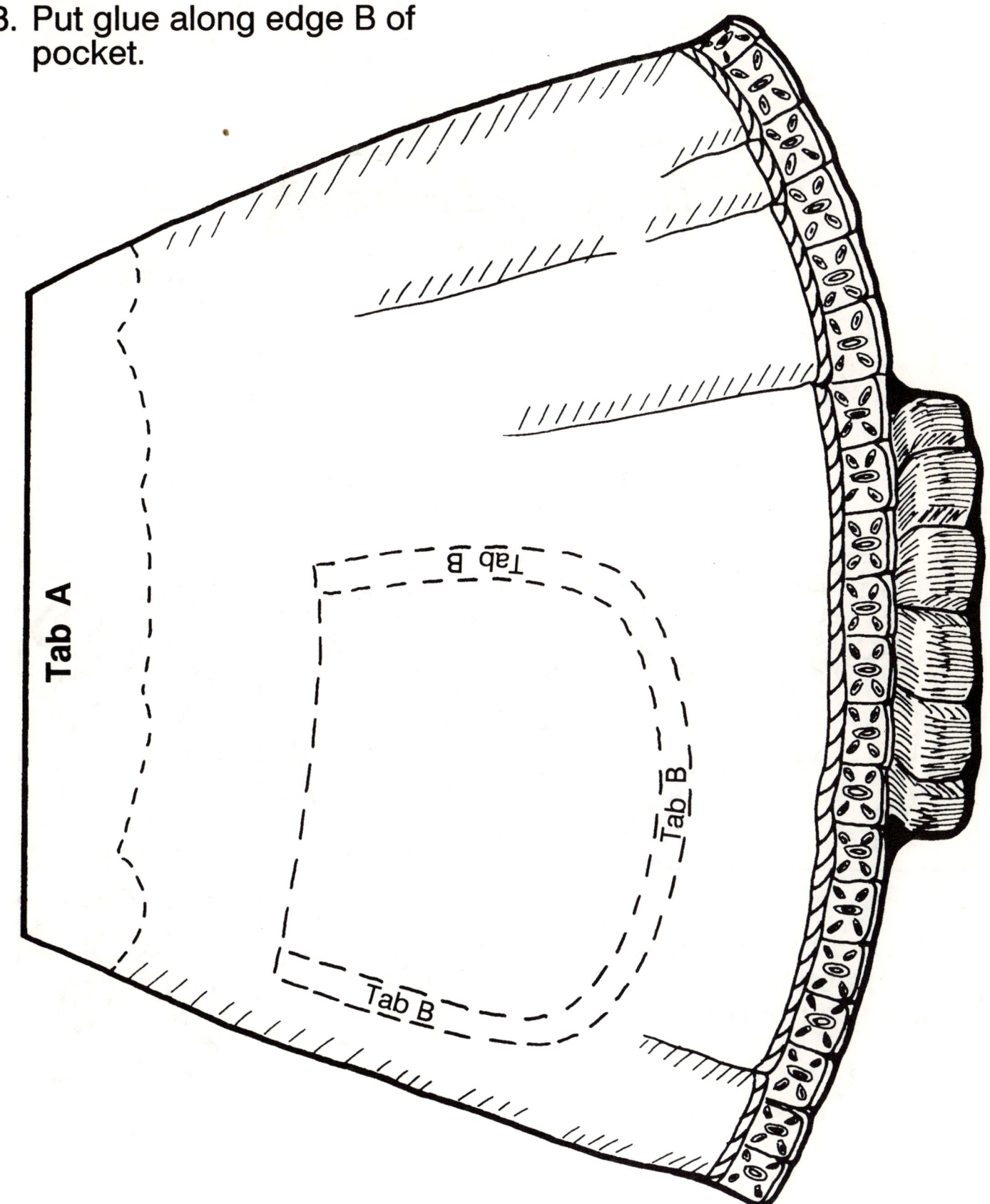

Name_____   *The Country Bunny and The Little Gold Shoes*

The Country Bunny *(cont.)*

4. Lay the "pocket" on top of Tab B.

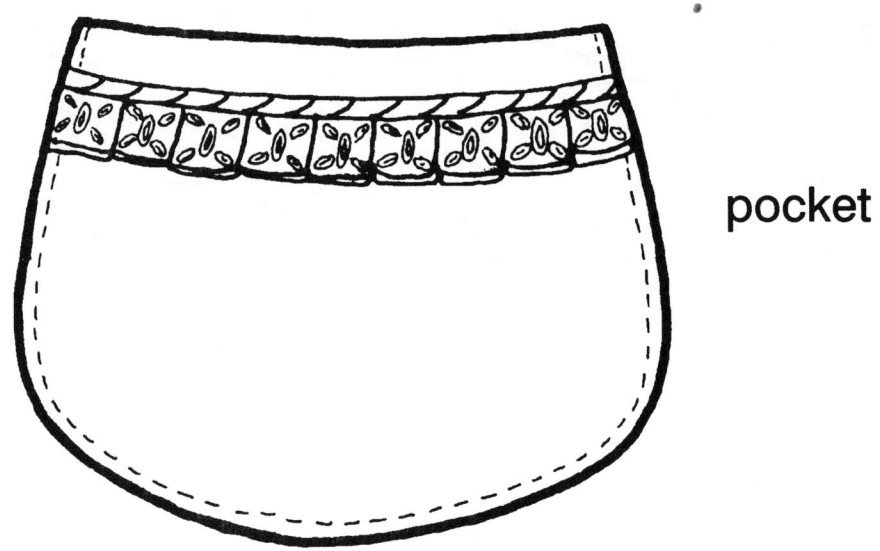

pocket

5. Cut out bunny cards. Sequence the cards in numerical order 1-21. Store cards in bunny's pocket.

Name _____ *The Country Bunny and The Little Gold Shoes*

The Country Bunny *(cont.)*

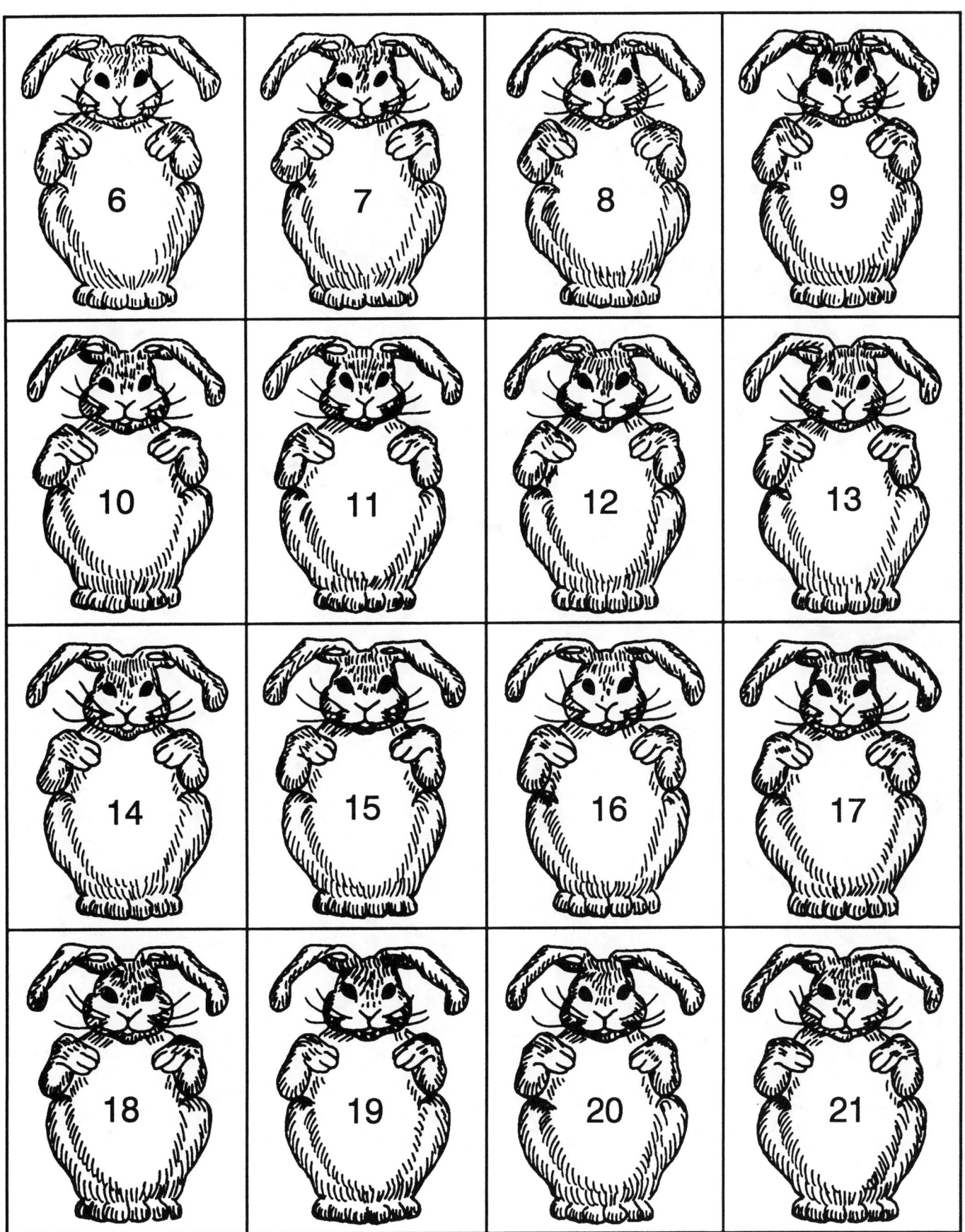

Name_____   *The Country Bunny and The Little Gold Shoes*

Golden Shoes And Eggs

1. Trace the dashes.
2. Color.

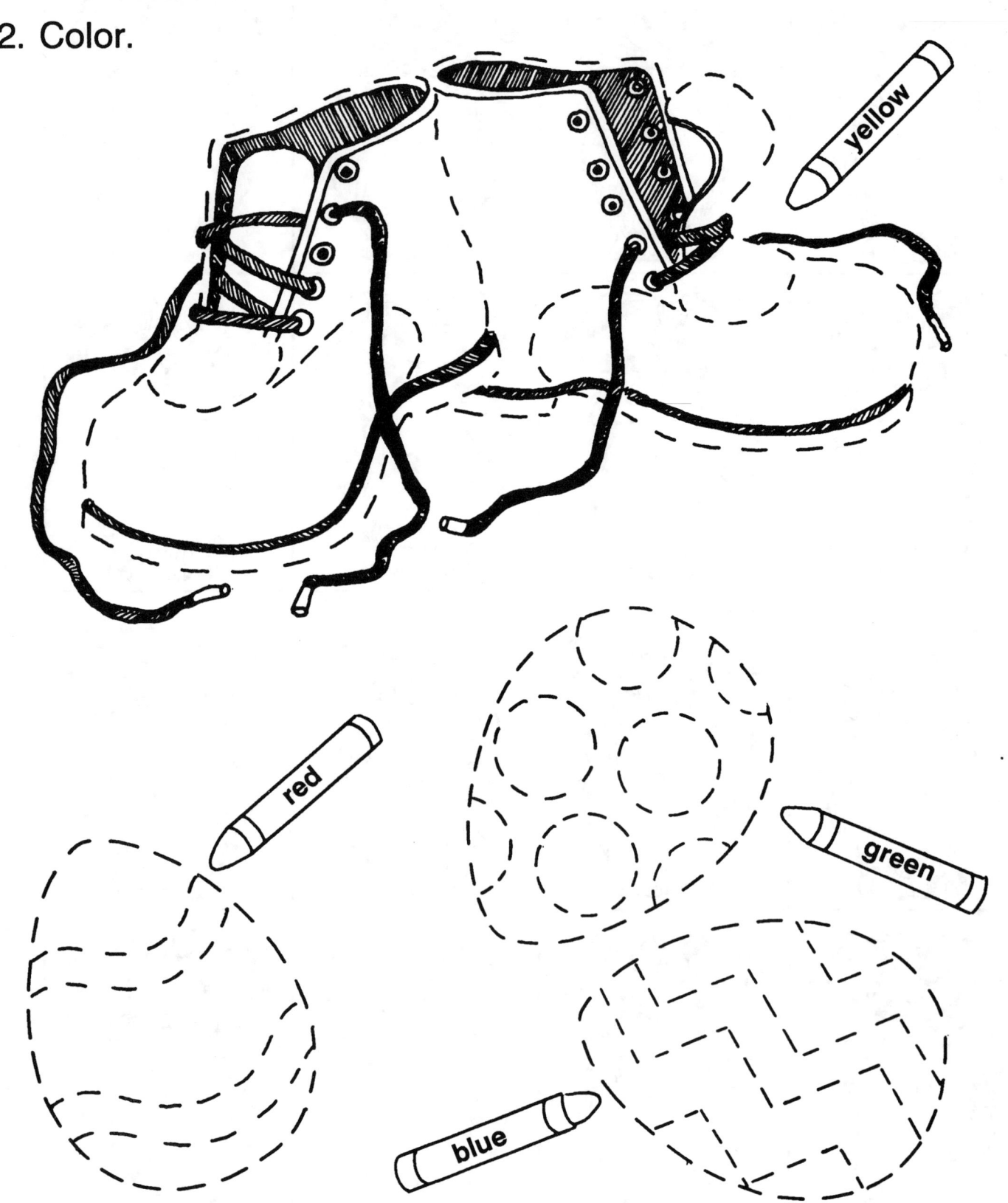

#304 Literature Activities For Young Children, Book 5   92   © 1990 Teacher Created Materials, Inc.

Name _____ *The Country Bunny and The Little Gold Shoes*

Mother Bunny

1. Connect the dots.
2. Color.

Name_____   *The Country Bunny and The Little Gold Shoes*

How Many Easter Eggs?

1. Count
2. Print numbers.
3. Color.

| 1 | 2 | |

#304 Literature Activities For Young Children, Book 5 — © 1990 Teacher Created Materials, Inc.

Name _____ *The Country Bunny and The Little Gold Shoes*

Bunny Clothes

*See suggested activity page 87.

© 1990 Teacher Created Materials, Inc. 95 #304 Literature Activities For Young Children, Book 5

Name_____ *The Country Bunny and The Little Gold Shoes*

Bunny Pattern

*See suggested activity page 87.

#304 Literature Activities For Young Children, Book 5   96   © 1990 Teacher Created Materials, Inc.